Black Women and the Changing Television Landscape

Black Women and the Changing Television Landscape

Lisa M. Anderson

BLOOMSBURY ACADEMIC
NEW YORK • LONDON • OXFORD • NEW DELHI • SYDNEY

BLOOMSBURY ACADEMIC
Bloomsbury Publishing Inc
1385 Broadway, New York, NY 10018, USA
50 Bedford Square, London, WC1B 3DP, UK
29 Earlsfort Terrace, Dublin 2, Ireland

BLOOMSBURY, BLOOMSBURY ACADEMIC and the Diana logo
are trademarks of Bloomsbury Publishing Plc

First published in the United States of America 2023

Cover images: (Clockwise from top right) Hattie McDaniel in a publicity still for the film,
Gone with the Wind, 1939. dir. Victor Fleming © Silver Screen Collection / Getty Images;
Woman watching TV © Getty Images; News reporter © Getty Images; Digital image of
woman interacting with screens © Getty Images; Viola Davis in a publicity shot from TV
series How to Get Away With Murder, 2014, Dir. Laura Innes © ABC STUDIOS / Album /
Alamy; Family watching TV © Getty Images

A catalog record for this book is available from the Library of Congress.

ISBN: HB: 978-1-5013-9362-4
         PB: 978-1-5013-9363-1
         ePDF: 978-1-5013-9365-5
         eBook: 978-1-5013-9364-8

Typeset by Integra Software Services Pvt. Ltd.
Printed and bound in the United States of America

To find out more about our authors and books visit www.bloomsbury.com
and sign up for our newsletters.

To the memories of Sarah Bryant-Bertail, who taught me semiotics and how to be a mentor, and Elsie G. J. Moore, who never stopped believing in what I could achieve.

Contents

List of Figures

Acknowledgments

Any book project ends up having many people who contribute to its development and writing. And a book that began as an idea more than a decade ago has many people to thank for its development.

First, I want to thank my colleagues at Arizona State University's School of Social Transformation, particularly my colleagues in Women and Gender Studies, for their support and understanding while I worked on this project. They generously listened while I prattled on about this project, and they talked about their own responses to many of the programs I discuss here. Particularly, I'm grateful for the opportunity to bounce ideas off Georgeanne Scheiner Gillis, Mako Fitts Ward, Marlon M. Bailey, and Michelle McGibbney Vlahoulis, whose own work in popular culture and performance helped me to refine my ideas, and gave me suggestions about other things I should watch and read. I'm also grateful for the support of SST colleagues Ersula Ore, Heather Switzer, and Karen Kuo. Thanks also to several of my current and former graduate students, especially Drs. Sakena Young-Scaggs, Cassandra M. Collier, and S. D. Bellamy, and current students Elisabeth Zoë Lacey and Kierra Otis, whose unflagging support buoyed me when I didn't feel this project was important. They guarded my time, nominated me for mentoring awards, and their discussions about the work pushed it in new directions. Thanks also to some of the senior faculty in the School whose support was instrumental. As Interim Director, Bryan Brayboy gave me time off from teaching to work on revisions, and both Mary Margaret Fonow and the late Elsie G. Moore, who served as School Directors before Bryan, supported me and this project in various ways.

I gave presentations on much of the material here at several conferences and talks. Thanks to the audience members from panels on which I presented this work at the National Women's Studies Association, Semiotic Society of America, and Caribbean Philosophical Association for valuable feedback and for asking questions that helped me deepen the work. Librarians at the Margaret Herrick Library, the Schomburg Center for Research in Black Culture, Fort Lauderdale African American Research Library and Cultural Center, and the New York Public Library helped me to access important documents and special collections, without which this project would not have been possible.

I owe a debt of gratitude to my editor, Katie Gallof, and her assistant Stephanie Grace-Patinos, who found me excellent reviewers who understood what I was doing and supported the book as it is. It can be challenging to find the right reviewers – especially at a time when so many people, especially in the humanities, are fatigued and people do not want to review manuscripts. It's been a blessing to work with you on the project. Thank you also to the anonymous reviewers whose recommendations at the end of this process were perfect.

There are several other people to whom I am deeply indebted. My developmental editor, Jennifer Quincey, worked with me through extensive revisions and made the manuscript bloom. My small group and mentor in the Faculty Success Program of the National Center for Faculty Diversity and Development helped me to stay on task, and provided me with the tools and strategies I needed to finish the manuscript revision. Thanks especially to my writing partner, Nicole Pagan, who kept me accountable for months as I finished drafts and worked revisions. Lewis R. Gordon, thank you for continuing to be a friend and mentor.

Finally, but by no means the least, I thank both my mom, M. Theresa Anderson, and my spouse Jacqueline Martinez, who supported me in all kinds of ways as I worked on this project in fits and starts. Mom read the first draft of the manuscript, and gave me important feedback from a sophisticated nonacademic reader. I always want to make sure that my work is not inaccessible to wider audiences, and Mom helps me be a clearer writer. Jackie convinced me that the project I had conceptualized more than a decade ago, which I had been told was "too narrow" because it only focused on Black women, was not too narrow, and was an important contribution to the field. I thank her for putting up with me through this project and all of the trials and tribulations that came along with it, for reading drafts at literally the last minute, and for watching episodes of television shows just for my research.

Introduction: An Ambivalent Relationship with Television

When I was growing up in the 1970s and 1980s, television was one of the times when the family did something together. My household was strongly focused on education, and my parents fostered our knowledge of Black history and literature, particularly because we lived in a white suburb. We were immersed in a wide range of popular culture, from music (jazz and R&B) to regular primetime television viewing. Having grown up in the South and mid-Atlantic, my parents were acutely aware of racism and stereotypes and the effects those stereotypes had on their children. I grew up reading Langston Hughes's and Nikki Giovanni's poetry and James Baldwin's novels, listening to Miles Davis and John Coltrane, and regularly viewing situation comedies that were popular at the time; we never missed an episode of *All in the Family* or *Good Times*, *Sanford and Son*, or *The Jeffersons*. We were glued to the television for *Roots*. And while we had a consciousness about negative stereotypes of Black people on television, we still watched when Black folk were on the TV.

As I grew older and became more acutely aware of the ways that these stereotypes about Blackness and Black people affected my everyday life, I looked at those programs with a more critical eye. As one of the few Blacks in my neighborhood or school, I was regularly subjected to an environment where (white) people asserted that I couldn't possibly live where I lived, that I would not be successful, and that I wasn't thought of by some as "really Black." These formative experiences shaped my intellectual curiosity, particularly as I have pondered the representations of Black women across cultural products (from novels to films). One might even say that it has been an abiding interest throughout my academic career. As I became a more critical reader and viewer, I saw that my early objections were less sophisticated. It was (and remains) easy to talk about "positive" and "negative" depictions of Blackness; for a time, it was easiest to talk about representation in somewhat simplistic terms. "Negative" depictions were those old racist stereotypes that showed Blackness as less-than, as animalistic, as ignorant, as superstitious, and on and on. My middle-class upbringing and aesthetics dictated that any "positive" representation would not be one that equated Blackness with poverty or criminality or buffoonery but one that today we might call "respectable," aligned with a "respectability politics" that believes that if we show sincere efforts at assimilation and "respectability," we will be accepted as "equal" by whites.[1]

As I was developing as a scholar, it seemed to me that what was seriously lacking, then, was a significant body of work aligned with this idea of respectability, which was often linked to racial uplift. My young interest in becoming a playwright was driven by my understanding of the need for scripts that spoke to Blackness and Black life, since so few seemed to exist. What I did not understand then was that there was already a body of that work; there had always been Black cultural production that entertained the variety of Black experiences. I just wasn't going to learn about it in a classroom. Then, as a graduate student, I discovered the wealth of cultural products by Black artists from the middle of the nineteenth century into contemporary periods, with bursts of productivity in the 1920s and the 1960s. Clearly, this work had been created and produced over decades. It just wasn't necessarily accessible to me. In addition, as my viewing became more critical, I noticed that different audiences engaged with these cultural products in very different ways. Even *Black* audiences did not receive these works in a uniform way. While *The Cosby Show* seemed to me universally liked among Black audiences, I would discover that this was not necessarily the case. I would also discover that white audiences deemed *The Cosby Show* an "unrealistic" depiction of Blacks in the United States.

Encountering the notion that *Cosby* was unrealistic was a defining moment in my early academic career. It remains a question that haunts me even as I continue to be as avid a consumer of the televisual as I am of the written word. It made me question what I thought of as a "positive" representation. Was it only because they were an upper-middle-class family, with educated parents, that we considered *Cosby* such a groundbreaking show? Could a show represent working-class Blackness and also be groundbreaking? What did it mean for a show to represent Blackness "positively"? And as my career continued, I began to encounter similar questions about representations of women (usually white women, but not always), couched in language of not only "positive" or "negative" but also of what things were or were not *feminist*, for a variety of reasons.

The thoughts around *Cosby*, and questions around "positive" and "negative" depictions, became the root of my ambivalence with the televisual. On the one hand, I enjoy and am entertained by television programming. I am attracted to good stories, good acting, and am especially smitten when the two come together. Moreover, I often feel the need to support the work of Black creatives, even when the product is lacking in story, acting, or both. My love of a "good" program sometimes means I will watch something that my critical mind finds "problematic," one that relies on two-dimensional characters or tired stereotypes. My love of seeing Black people on television means that sometimes I will watch something that isn't great. Sometimes, it's a genre that doesn't appeal to me—I am not a fan of horror as a genre, and typically avoid those programs, although sometimes I will try for the sake of (again) supporting a Black-themed show (*Lovecraft Country* was this for me; I was able to watch a few episodes but could not finish it). I also find it difficult, and traumatizing, to watch depictions of Black pain and death (unless the story and the acting can carry me through the trauma). Realistic and honest as they may be, and as *important* as they are for the viewing public to witness, I sometimes cannot watch. My viewing habits reflect this ambivalence; the programs I watch as I turn off my critical eye, and those I watch begrudgingly because I feel I "should," and the programs that truly bring me joy and allow me to revel in the wonderful beauty of the worlds of Black creatives.

My critical lens is explicitly Black feminist cultural critique, and this is how I consider the specific representations of Black people, and especially Black women, that have consumed me over the course of my career. My influences here include bell hooks, Patricia Hill Collins, Michelle Wallace, Jacqueline Bobo, and Audre Lorde (Bobo 1995; Collins 1990, 2005; hooks 1992; Lorde 1983; Wallace 2004). But I have also realized while becoming more engaged with these arts that it is not as simple as "positive" or "negative," "feminist" or not. To simply say that a television program is a positive or negative representation assumes all kinds of values and judgment, aesthetic considerations, and cultural knowledge. This is not to say that there are not egregiously racist representations of Blackness in the media; there have been, and they persist to the current moment. It is to say that representation is complex, and how we come to take up or view a given representation may be through an oppositional reading, to use Stuart Hall's notion (1993) and bell hooks's Black feminist usage (1992). We may also take images up in an uncritical way, without questioning how they take on meaning in the broader US culture, especially among nonblack people. We may take them up in both ways, at different times, deriving pleasure from a text that may reinforce racist views of Black people. One of the goals of this project, then, is to rethink how we consider representations, how we situate them in cultural moments, and how those moments come to have meaning for us.

There was one other impetus for this text. Asked to write a biographical entry for Thelma "Butterfly" McQueen, I delved into the life and work of this actor who was most infamous for the roles she played, especially Prissy in *Gone with the Wind*. An assessment of McQueen's body of work, and the challenges she faced when she chose to stop playing the stereotypical roles available to her in Hollywood, led me to rewatch *Gone with the Wind*. What I saw this time was not the stereotyped portrayal most people see when they watch (and object to) the film. I began to wonder how McQueen's performance might be read oppositionally: if we thought of her not as acquiescing to racist portrayals of Black women but as embodying a trickster figure. What emerged for me in that moment was a way of seeing Prissy not as Margaret Mitchell and Sidney Howard wrote her but as McQueen played her. It made a space to consider McQueen's portrayal of Prissy as a kind of trickster figure in the mold of Black folklore tales of Ole John and Massa, or Brer Rabbit. Reading Prissy this way also led me to reconsider Hattie McDaniel's equally denigrated performance as Mammy, and indeed the Mammy roles about which I wrote early in my career. The documentary video about the making of *Gone with the Wind* notably contains an interview of McQueen, in which she recalls going to David O. Selznick with other Black cast members to object to explicitly racist elements in the script and the novel. They convinced him to change some of that material. How often did this happen, that Black actors were able to use their influence to change the nature of the films (or television programs) of which they were a part?

Considering McDaniel's award-winning performance led me to *The Beulah Show*, which captured my interest as the first television series that featured a Black female protagonist. *Beulah* had originally been a radio program, like *Amos 'N' Andy*, and like *Amos 'N' Andy*, it featured a cast of white men who played the roles of Black characters. Both *Beulah* and *Amos 'N' Andy* are typically seen as the transformation of blackface minstrelsy with white actors from vaudeville into radio. *Beulah* would go through two major transformations: it would, after the death of the white man who read Beulah, hire a Black woman to replace him; and it would transition from the radio to the emergent medium of television. These two shifts created in the program interesting potential, even if that potential was never fully achieved. When *The Beulah Show* was cancelled, it would be more than a decade before another television program with a Black female protagonist appeared. Pondering *The Beulah Show* led me to consider more television programming featuring Black women. In this I consider how they were represented and what kind of a say they might have had in that representation. What would it take for Black women to appear on the small screen, in vehicles designed for them, in ways that better reflected the lives of Black women specifically, and Black people generally?[2]

Considering the Television Landscape

Ultimately, this project is concerned with four questions or ideas. They are not necessarily "research questions" per se, but they are the ideas that persist through my interest in television and representation.

First is the idea of black aesthetics and the tension between those who wish to see the variety of black life and experience represented and those who remain interested in representing the "best" of black life. Deeply entrenched within these arguments is the fact of creating representations within a white supremacist system. Contestations among Black artists and scholars reflect these arguments; they were, for example, the core of the intellectual conflict between W. E. B. DuBois and Alain Locke in the 1920s. Locke's interest in the cultural products of Blacks, which represented a range of their lived experiences, clashed with DuBois's belief that art must serve a *political* end and must actively counter depictions of Blacks as anything other than "respectable." These two perspectives on the contested terrain of Black performance (and aesthetics) in a white supremacist culture have long dominated discussions about both Black aesthetics and Black performance (Elam and Krasner 2001; Harrison 1972; Hay 1994; Hill 1987; Mitchell 1967). These are also part of the discussion about Black representation on television. The difference between, say, a "Beulah" and a "Julia" is not merely a matter of class representation; it is also a matter of whether a representation seems mired in racist caricature (Beulah) or whether it shows the "best" of us, such as a respectable middle-class "lady" (Julia). In that context, I wonder: For Black audiences, what makes an "acceptable" representation, and does that change over time? Do we read oppositionally, and if we do, do we still hesitate about roles that embrace a white imaginary of Blackness? When programming is protested, what grounds that protest?

The second of the guiding ideas surrounds the politics and economics of what gets produced and under what circumstances. At one level, this is a question of who has access to the means of production (for television through the years has required a substantial investment from a studio for both production and distribution). There are questions about what kinds of projects are funded or supported by studios and which ones are not. On another level, when we consider the intersections of aesthetics (particularly in a white supremacist system) and political economy, we begin to get a sense of what things sell, and what things do not, within and to the dominant culture. While television ratings do not wholly determine a program's longevity anymore, whether a targeted audience watches does still influence sponsors and studios (be they ABC or Amazon) about continuing a given program. As I discuss in detail beginning in Chapter 4, the diversification of outlets has significantly changed television consumption for the average viewer. We might conclude, after seeing the changes in representation from the mid-1990s to today, that what ends up on "television" and how it represents people (particularly Black people, but other underrepresented groups, as well) is partially determined by who has access to production and who produces. The things that determine what is renewed and what is cancelled have shifted over time, but is that shift necessarily good? When a Black person owns a television network—early BET (Black Entertainment Television) or the current OWN (Oprah Winfrey Network)—is the programming significantly different? Does it function under the same aesthetic strictures (respectability vs. variety) as programming on white-owned networks? And if Oprah can do what she wants, what does that look like, and is it good for viewers in general, and Black people in particular?

A third overarching consideration is what circumstances enable representation to become more diversified, to have more verisimilitude, and to represent as much of a range of Blackness as there is of whiteness in the world of the televisual. This is intimately related to the questions of ownership of the means of production, but is also a way to consider what the significant and substantial changes in television programming—both expansions and contractions—have meant for representations of Blackness and Black women. There have been two major expansions of television outlets; the first, in the 1990s, with additional cable channels offering original programming, and another more recent change that includes streaming content, user-developed content, and technologies (digital and cloud-based recording) that have substantially changed the way people watch "television." Do these expansions and diversifications generate significant and lasting changes in representations? If a long-standing argument against the portrayal of Black people as living only in the inner city and in poverty was that it became the predominant way of viewing Blackness and Black people, do those same arguments hold when different representations are available to audiences? As I explore in Chapter 1, so much of the opposition to *The Beulah Show* by Blacks in the 1950s was the fact that the title character was a maid in a white household. The paucity of representations at the time—there was *Beulah*, and *Amos 'N' Andy*, and not much else—meant that the only televisual representations of Blackness codified a certain kind of Blackness in a way that both appealed to, and was recognizable to, white audiences. This type of representation—what Patricia Hill Collins calls "controlling images"—resonates through the "real" world and has consequences for the everyday lives of Black folk; as she argues, these representations have material effects on law and public policy (1990).

Is it simply a question of critical mass? In other words, does it matter less if some representations are stereotypical if there are enough representations that the stereotypical ones do not become iconic of Blackness? If so, how do we get there? If that is not the answer to bringing a diversity of Blackness to the world of the televisual, what is? And if representations have changed since the days of Beulah and Amos, what kinds of things had to be in place for those changes to happen?

Thus we come to the final of the considerations. In a way, this question is one that has fueled this project since I began thinking about it in the early 2000s. If Butterfly McQueen and other actors were able to convince David O. Selznick to change some of the worst of *Gone with the Wind*, were there other circumstances in which this could happen? And, if so, was it possible that an actor's reputation could allow for them to wield sufficient power in writing, directing, and producing television programs that they could be a driving force for change within television? What Black women actors—particularly those who had crossed from successful stage careers to television—made changes in their television roles in part because of their influence?

In the theatre world, production is a collaboration between the different roles: director, designers, actors, and sometimes writers, as well. Actors work collaboratively with the director on things like what their character—as they have developed it through script study—might or might not do, how they might say lines, and, if they are working in development with a new script, whether their character would say a particular line or word. Collaborating is part of the theatrical process, and it is this process of feedback to the director (and writers) that I saw in that early instance in *Gone with the Wind*, where the Black actors influenced Selznick to make significant changes to the script. I wondered whether actors in *television* might have some of the same influence or ability to shape those works, as well.

I argue that the theatre–TV connection is that actors who come from a theatrical background are more accustomed to articulating these kinds of changes to scripts, characters, and even plots, and expecting that their opinions—because they come from a deep engagement with the character— are taken seriously. There is also a kind of political consciousness among many of the profiled actors about the implications of representations, and because of that consciousness, a desire to change them or make them "better" in some way.

"Negotiating" Hollywood

There are many different types of representations that I could consider, even within the televisual realm. But in this work, I am interested in what kinds of things allow for, or push, these representations in different ways; what it takes to make meaningful change in Black television characters and programming, and what those representations might look like. As a semiotician, I am focused on how the various elements of the texts (image and script) create meanings, and how those meanings are taken up within both broader and more specific communities.

I am also interested in the representations of Black *women*. This is not to say that Black masculinity has not been subject to the same stresses and pressures as Black femininity; it is to say that while these types of representation are tied to each other, the representation of Black women is my primary concern. As this project emerges from my own intersectional Black feminism, the representations of Black women are also tied to the representations of Black *families*, for several reasons. Depictions of Black women who did not have families of their own, which frequently happens in the "Black maid/mammy" characters, were strongly critiqued as not representative of the lives of Black women who worked as domestics. In addition, Black single-parent families headed by women perpetuate negative views of Black women. Therefore, the representation of families is intimately tied to representations of Black women.

I chose to examine shows that would be considered "Black-themed" or in which, even in a more ensemble program, a Black woman was a primary character if not the main character. This meant that ensemble programs that might have included a Black cast member, but whose subject matter was not focused on the Black (female) character, were operating in a different kind of aesthetic. This excluded many interesting representations of Black women; for example, Nichelle Nichols's groundbreaking role on *Star Trek* (the original series) would not be included, because Nichols was not a lead character. Also not included are the many programs from the 1980s through the 2010s that are ensemble procedural dramas (police, law, and hospital shows). Aside from a couple of short-lived exceptions, Black families are mostly found on one particular genre in television: the situation comedy. As Robin Means Coleman said, "if I want to write about African Americans as stars in their own shows, then Black situation comedies *had* to be the target genre" (1998, 3).

Working with the sitcom as a genre is compelling for multiple reasons. Situation comedy spans the entire period of television, much of which moved from radio programs (*Beulah* is an example of this) in the early years, but became a staple of television through its broadcast heyday. Some of the most successful, long-running programs in television history have been situation comedies. Their half-hour format makes them profitable for networks; they cost less to produce than hour-long programs. Audiences can tune in weekly to see the latest antics of their favorite characters. Comedy has the potential to make pointed social commentary in ways that are more palatable to audiences. While the first Black-white interracial kiss was on a science fiction show (*Star Trek*), other firsts, like discussion of abortion, homosexuality, HIV/AIDS, and other compelling issues, have been material for the sitcom (*Maude, Soap, A Different World*, respectively).

Sitcoms are also worth examining because on the whole, with a few exceptions, they are set in *domestic* or *private* spaces (Entman and Rojecki 2000). Typically, they are set within the private space of the household, and because the United States is a segregated society in which interracial marriage only became legal nationally in 1969 (*Loving v. Virginia*), the sitcom is a space in which there has historically been little integration. Occasionally, Black people pop into white private spaces; Florida Evans, as Maude's maid, is one such example (until she got her own show). Sitcoms, therefore, reflect our society particularly as they show us how domestic spaces exist, and how segregation *persists*, across time. Rarely are sitcoms integrated, and ones that are typically use a public space as the setting (*The Office* and *30Rock* are two recent examples). Others may be located in private spaces, but Black characters who enter those spaces do so as employees—so it is still a public space for the Black character (e.g., *Maude*, *Benson*). Ensemble shows and hour-long dramas that take place in public spaces (the myriad hospital and police procedurals especially) do tend be integrated, because those spaces are integrated, particularly in recent decades. However, even there, as Entman and Rojecki have shown, the integration is limited; Black characters are depicted in supervisory roles, giving them fewer opportunities to engage with their majority-white employees on whom the programs center. They refer to this phenomenon as a "utopian reversal," wherein, "as one might expect, hierarchy defeats verbal expression of intimacy, defined here as self-disclosure by the Black character. Formal, role-bound exchanges are the rule in two-thirds of interracial relationships where Blacks appear as superiors to Whites, matched by 60 percent of those in which Blacks are subordinated to Whites" (2000, 154).

Since these programs seldom if ever focus on the interior (private) lives of the Black characters they include, the grounding for much of this project lies in the situation comedy, for if we want to look at Black women embedded in families and communities, that is where we will find them. However, the hour-long drama tends to be the place where there is more verisimilitude, or at least the potential for it. That television has not been willing to "risk" an hour-long domestic drama featuring a Black family means that while we might cite programs that feature the interior lives of white (usually middle-class) characters, a similar program for Black audiences was not sustainable until recently (as we will consider in Chapter 5).

To see how Black women performed various types of negotiation with Hollywood, this project focuses primarily on situation comedies in which Black women play a central or leading role (where they are, for the most part, the central character). I selected one program per decade. In the first two decades of broadcast television, there was little choice. *The Beulah Show* was the only Black woman-headed situation comedy in the 1950s, and *Julia* stood alone during the 1960s. My exploration into *Beulah* made me curious about what kinds of potential *influence* the "stars" of these programs had on the writing, story lines, and direction. These women were both objects of the camera's gaze (in a very different way than white women were objects of that gaze, which was often sexualizing) and central to the program; without Diahann Carroll, there was no *Julia*. What influence might they have had on the productions? In the

1970s, there emerge more possibilities, but among all of them, we have Esther Rolle, veteran of the Negro Ensemble Company and experienced stage actor, who has the potential to expand the representation of Black people on television. Of all of the options, *Good Times* combines the "star" quality of an experienced stage actor and a producer who seems to, as John Amos said, have "his finger on the pulse of America" (2014). Despite this, all of these programs eventually ran afoul of Black audiences and organizations, who spoke out against each program in turn. Something still wasn't quite right in these programs, and more recent developments in the field may give us some reasons why.

The work of these women actors generates yet another question: If we cannot make change in front of the camera, what happens when we move behind it? What is revealed about Black life when programs are guided by a Black feminist sensibility? In other words, when the concern is for representing the diversity of Blackness, and more specifically Black womanhood, what does that look like, and what emerges? How do audiences—both Black audiences and broader audiences—connect with the programs? In fact, much work published on Black television considers Black audiences, examining how they feel about the work that is said to represent them on the small screen (Coleman 1998; Smith-Shomade 2002). Other work focuses on representations (Gray 2004). Some work focuses on genre, such as Adilifu Nama's work on Black representation in science fiction films and Bambi Haggins's work on comedy (Haggins 2007; Nama 2008). In this text, while I do attend to the representations themselves and how they offer (or try to offer) different kinds of Blackness, I am also interested in the possibilities and limits of actor influence and the importance both of Blacks in production and of diversification of media outlets. This work sits among texts such as Christine Acham's *Revolution Televised* (2004) and Kristal Brent Zook's *Color by Fox!* (1999), which also take up the complex object that is Blackness in network television, considering texts as well as audiences and cultural contexts. I argue that it is only when there is a critical mass of programming that we truly begin to see a diversification of Black representation, something that is outside of the white imaginary of Blackness. Only when those producing these programs—not exclusively women, but with a critical mass of Black women producers and showrunners—have a keen interest in the social, cultural, and political effects of representation will television broadcast the breadth and depth of Black lives and talent. And finally, the writing has to reflect the broad diversity of Blackness in ways that ring true to Black audiences.

Chapter 1 explores the phenomenon of *The Beulah Show* and its mostly well-known actors. In this chapter, biographical materials, archival materials including scripts and letters, and television episodes provide the core materials. Key to this analysis is not only examining some of the television program's episodes but also deeply considering the problematics of the program and how its "stars" may have contributed to the groundswell of Black resistance to the show. Thus, this chapter presents the careers of Ethel Waters, Hattie McDaniel, and Louise Beavers, the three major actors who portrayed Beulah on the small screen. It also explores the radio program on which the television program was based and demonstrates how Hattie McDaniel worked to intervene and shift representations within the confines of 1940s radio and 1950s television.

In Chapter 2 I consider the Diahann Carroll vehicle, *Julia*. A departure from the maid and mammy representations that dominated the small screen in the 1950s, *Julia* attempts to represent the Black middle class. Carroll's career as a stage and film actor is an important element, as is her Black middle-class upbringing. Carroll's autobiography, interviews, and episodes of *Julia* compose the material for the historical and critical analysis. There were high hopes for a program that starred a Black woman who did not work as a maid. In this chapter, then, I focus on some of the episodes that seem typical of the show's efforts around representations of Blackness and the show's politics (or rather the politics of Hal Kanter, the show's creator). The development of the program, and access to Carroll's memories of working on the show, bolsters the analysis and contributes to understanding why *Julia* did not live up to its initial promise.

In the 1970s we are finally treated to a situation comedy that features a Black nuclear family. In that, *Good Times* is perhaps even more the program that Black audiences wanted. Set in the Cabrini-Green housing projects (before they would become known for violence in the early 1980s), James and Florida Evans and their children J. J., Thelma, and Michael would become the working-class Black family that, at least in theory, Black audiences were waiting for. *Good Times* was a spin-off of *Maude*, which itself was a spin-off of *All in the Family* and part of Norman Lear's 1970s dynasty of television sitcoms. Once again, we have an experienced stage actor (Rolle, who acted for years with the Negro Ensemble Company) who had a consciousness about Black art and culture and might have had some influence over how the family was represented; after all, Lear wanted the family to be fatherless, and Rolle insisted that not be the case. Archival material, newspaper articles, interviews, and other secondary sources ground this chapter's exploration of the show and Rolle as an actor. The end of the 1970s would come, and *Good Times* would be gone; this chapter explores some of the reasons why, yet again, Black viewers protested, and it lost viewership until it was cancelled.

The late 1980s would finally see Black sitcom programming that was *different* from what had come before. Chapter 4 explores the most groundbreaking of these sitcoms, *A Different World*, through episodes as well as interviews and articles about Debbie Allen. Yet again, an experienced Black woman would be instrumental in the show developing as it did; this chapter also marks the turning point where, having modest success through the influence of skilled actors, we begin to see Black women working as "showrunners," with roles in writing, directing, and producing. This represents a significant change both in representations and in how Black audiences relate to what we might call "Black-themed" programs. I argue that having a Black woman showrunner is one element of the shift that happens in the late 1980s and through the 1990s; the other element is the diversification of media outlets. The emergence of Fox as a major network and the mentoring of young Black talent in writing, directing, and producing would bring us the other program highlighted in this chapter, *Living Single*. These two programs, while not focused on families per se, would stand as major changes in television representation.

Chapter 5 focuses attention on the work of four Black women showrunners and creators in the first two decades of the twenty-first century. I focus on the work of Shonda Rhimes, Mara Brock Akil, Issa Rae, and Ava DuVernay. These four women have made significant inroads into television production; their programs vary and include sitcoms (the Black sitcom focused not on families, but on mostly young(ish) Black professionals in their daily lives), ensemble multiracial programs, and finally, a Black family drama. During this time we will see both an extension of the type of programming that emerged and became popular in the 1990s and major technological changes that would also push change (both in diversification of outlets and in talent) in the second decade. What emerges in the 2000s and 2010s is a logical extension of the work from the 1990s, particularly as the project of mentoring younger people establishes a pool of successful people on which networks are willing to take risks.

I conclude with a return to the actor, but in this case, the actor is not confined to only acting. Engaging with the work, both in front of and behind the camera, of Viola Davis and Regina King, I explore the culmination of decades of work by Black women in television, both as actors and as showrunners, and argue that their award-winning performances in theatre, television, and film made it possible for them to substantially advocate for Black-themed programming. I also point to emerging voices, particularly Janelle Monáe, whose work spans music, film, and television, and Marsai Martin, who has engaged with mentors and is charting a path that already includes producing.

Fighting the Stereotypes, 1948–52:
The Beulah Show and Its Actors

By the 1930s, the standard stereotypes of Black women had been largely codified, brought into film through the theatre and vaudeville circuits that began in the 1820s with the dawn of Blackface minstrelsy (Anderson 1997). Even though there was and had been a countertradition of Blacks performing Blackface minstrelsy from the mid-nineteenth century on (Anderson 1995; Bean 2001; Bean, Hatch, and McNamara 1996; Taylor and Austen 2012; Toll 1974), the politics and challenges of that countertradition were unable to radically transform the stereotypes and caricatures of Blackness that prevailed in theatre and performance in the United States. To understand the industry as it stood in the 1950s, we must recognize that these stereotypes were deeply ingrained in the white American cultural imagination. The image of Aunt Jemima, and all of the various film mammies from *Birth of a Nation*'s Blackface mammy to Louise Beavers's Aunt Delilah, was standard fare and standard stock characters in all of the representational arts (Morrison 1992). The dogged persistence of these types of roles continues to the current day; however, to some degree they are challenged in subtle and not-so-subtle ways. The recent horror film *Ma*, starring Octavia Spencer, uses the mammy and her iconicity but turns the icon on its head by creating a character who might have been understood as a benevolent mammy but is actually a killer.

Thus opportunities for Black actors remained limited in the early decades of film, and the scarcity that marked the world of television when it debuted in the late 1940s continued until the recent past. As we move through the decades, we will begin to see that what emerges of Blackness in television—like what emerged in theatre, in radio, and in film—resided strongly within a white-centered world in which Blacks were not and could not be central. As Miriam Petty notes, "a speaking role with any significant screen time, or a character who could boast of any depth or dimensionality, was an exceptional, phenomenal occurrence, one that happened just frequently enough to stoke the hopes of the very ambitious" (2016, 4). Black actors in film were subject to the same constraints as Black actors in the theatre, largely "constrained by the larger racialized structure of the American film industry itself" (Petty 2016, 5). Black actors were faced with the necessity of negotiating *whether* to act, knowing that these were the very limited roles to which they had access, and if they did, whether there was an opportunity for them to subvert or reshape the role into one of which they could be proud, relatively.

While these stereotyped roles were engrained in the cultural imagination, with deep-set cultural meanings, they also still held a possibility of resistance within them. Others have also argued for a deeper, more critical understanding of some of the performances of these roles as satire, at least in the minds of the Black actors who were required to perform them if they wanted to work in the industry (Bean et al. 1996; Petty 2016; Watts 2005). One example of this kind of satiric performance was the tradition of the cakewalk.[1] We can see both how the Black performers envisioned and enacted the cakewalk as satire and how simultaneously white audiences viewed it as a quaint approximation of white performance. I am arguing here for the possibility and reality, particularly through this period that begins with Bert Williams and George Walker's breakthrough in vaudeville (1896, with the musical *The Gold Bug*), that both counterperformance and oppositional reading were employed by Black performers and audiences.

In the 1930s, as film begins its meteoric rise (along with the rise of the "movie star"), films that depicted domestic settings often included Blacks as maids and butlers. These films were written and directed by white creators, and thus written from a perspective that was unfamiliar with Black American cultures; we will see this as a theme in television production. The characters were, and could only be, written from a perspective that only ever saw the surface life of Blacks and was also unable to see or understand when that surface was a mask. In addition, it is necessary to acknowledge that television, the primary focus of this book, drew from the film studios that preceded and coexisted with it, and that there was and remains heavy cross-pollination across media and performance (including theatre). While there were actors whose experience was only in film, many had their early training in the theatre, including not only Ethel Waters and Hattie McDaniel but other famous Black actors of the period, such as Paul Robeson (Eugene O'Neil's *The Emperor Jones*), Fredi Washington (her first role was in the Black musical *Shuffle Along*), and Thelma "Butterfly" McQueen (danced with Katherine Dunham and appeared in plays on Broadway, including *What a Life* in 1938).

Black performers, especially those who were steeped in the theatrical traditions, were not only well aware of the stereotypes of the white imaginary but sought, in ways that they could, to challenge and contradict those stereotypes. Awareness of the types of "doubling" that were endemic to the Black live performance traditions of the late nineteenth and early twentieth centuries (minstrelsy, vaudeville, and early Black musical theatre) was, I argue here, also present at times in these early representations. Certainly Lincoln Perry (Stepin Fetchit) created a performance that is precisely the type I refer to here; his acting "made him the apotheosis of the 1930s chief African American racial stereotype—as well as a blatant parody thereof, for those able and willing to see his performance as such" (Petty 2016, 7). But unlike in the Black audiences who watched vaudeville performances and knew to see the wink and nod in the cakewalk, film and television were not watched with the same kinds of oppositional readings that were present, and easy, in what were all-Black settings. It was also more difficult to insert these types of rebellious performances into films and television programs where white writers and directors had control over the final product and could edit out moments that did not make sense to them.

In a context so restrictive, where Black actors were occasionally able to "steal the show" or win an Academy Award for Best Supporting Actress, it is clear from the larger conversation within Black communities and Black intellectual circles that the tension between respectability and verisimilitude remained a concern in early film, and that this transition followed these actors onto the small screen. When there is resistance to these roles (such as the letter-writing campaigns against programs like *Amos 'N' Andy* and *The Beulah Show*), it is primarily because the depictions of these Black characters lack respectability; but arguments that these roles also lacked verisimilitude can also be supported. In other words, these characters that emerged from the white imaginary could not help but fail to reflect Black lives.

There is also the fact of these programs' popularity. The shows were popular with white audiences, who were comfortable seeing Blacks in these stereotyped roles. *Amos 'N' Andy* ranked in the top thirty programs in the Nielsen rankings for two of its seasons (1951–2 and 1952–3), and while *Beulah* never made it to the top thirty, its long radio history speaks to its popularity (and it might have earned higher ratings with McDaniel in the lead role, as the episodes she made were not broadcast during the program's first run) (Brooks and Marsh 2007).[2] It is worth noting that in 1951, the number of households with a television was around

12 percent (Riggs 1992); while a small percentage that would grow over time, television was still an emergent medium. When we consider things like Nielsen rankings for programs during this period, it is important to remember what a small percentage of the population is watching *televisions* at this point in history. As televisions would become more popular and more affordable in subsequent decades, viewers would see many of the programs of the 1950s as reruns. Their impact as visual representations of Blackness would reverberate well beyond the early 1950s. Finally, the addition of a Black actor to play Beulah created advertising opportunities that had been previously impossible; with an actual person to be Beulah, advertisers could use a "real" Beulah's image to sell products.

In the chapter that follows, I examine parts of the careers of three Black women actors who were successful within the film industry from the 1930s to the 1950s and who made, even if only briefly, the transition to television. I will review their film (and theatre) careers, but the chapter will focus on their work on *The Beulah Show,* as the first television series that featured a Black female protagonist. I chose *The Beulah Show* for several reasons. First, and most obviously, it was the first television program to feature a Black woman lead character. It had originally been a radio program, like *Amos 'N' Andy* (radio 1928–55, television 1951–3), and like *Amos 'N' Andy*, it featured a cast of white men who played the roles of Black characters. Both *Beulah* and *Amos 'N' Andy* are typically seen as the transformation of Blackface minstrelsy with white actors from vaudeville into radio (Ely 1991). *Beulah* would go through two major transformations; it would, after the death of the white man who read Beulah, hire a Black woman to replace him, and it would transition from the radio to the emergent medium of television. These two transformations created in the program interesting potential, even if that potential was never fully achieved. When *The Beulah Show* ended, it would be more than a decade before there would be another television program with a Black female protagonist.

I was able to access only five television episodes of *The Beulah Show*; one with Ethel Waters, two with Hattie McDaniel, and two with Louise Beavers. While this is a severely limited pool of episodes, they do give a strong idea of what the show was like.

Hattie McDaniel began the radio show in 1947. Ethel Waters worked on the show from its transition from radio to television from 1950 to 1952. McDaniel later replaced Waters in 1952, but completed only six episodes before her illness forced her to leave the show. Louise Beavers replaced McDaniel and continued in the role until the show ended in 1953. The radio show continued until 1954 (it ran longer than the television program), with two other actors taking on the role of Beulah after McDaniel's death. All three women were both famous (or infamous) for portraying mammy characters in films from the 1930s through the 1940s. First, we will discuss the iconic roles for Waters, McDaniel, and Beavers, then discuss their portrayals of Beulah. Finally, we will consider the politics, aesthetics, and the effects these actors had on the role of Beulah.

Black Female Roles of the 1930s

Much has been written about the stereotyped roles that predominated in the 1930s in film for Black women (Anderson 1997; Bogle 1996; Jewell 1993; Wallace 1990). I argue in part that the primary reason Waters, McDaniel, and Beavers could be cast as Beulah was that their significant careers and name recognition during the 1930s and 1940s allowed them to be the kind of "household" names that would help ensure an initial television audience. A transition from radio to television did not necessarily guarantee a new audience, and the radio program would continue even while the television show premiered, ran, and faltered. All three actors had significant film and/or stage careers during this period, and all demonstrate a level of success (marked here by being hired for multiple films over the decade) within the confines of Hollywood film. I will argue that their relative fame in Hollywood allowed them to have some influence over the performance and characterization of Beulah; while ultimately inadequate, it demonstrates that Black actors did wield some modicum of power in Hollywood. Their work on this program marks the transition into a new medium and a potential to make Black representation different.

Ethel Waters had a significant music and stage career before being cast as Beulah, and in fact, she did *Beulah* at the same time as performing on Broadway in *Member of the Wedding* (Bogle 2011). Waters had also performed in two well-known films of the 1940s, *Cabin in the Sky* and *Pinky*, which gave her name recognition by 1950, when the television series was first cast. Hattie McDaniel's career was "made" by her performance and Academy Award for *Gone with the Wind*, but she had performed in vaudeville for years prior to getting into film, and she had twenty-seven uncredited roles before she made her mark with *Gone with the Wind*. Two other notable appearances were "Queenie" in *Show Boat* in 1936 and "Aunt Tempy" in *Song of the South* in 1946. Louise Beavers acted in 106 films between 1929 and 1940; usually, she was playing a maid.

Ethel Waters

Ethel Waters, like Hattie McDaniel, had a long career on the stage (and in Waters's case, also in music performance) before coming to the small screen. Waters's career began in vaudeville, like McDaniel's, but for Waters, this was initially in music, specifically the blues. Her Broadway career began with the musical *Africana* in 1927, and while the show itself was not a critical success, it was Waters's Broadway debut (Bogle 2011). Waters performed on Broadway in the 1930s and at the Cotton Club, as well. *Beulah* was not her first venture into television; in 1939, NBC broadcast the fifteen-minute *The Ethel Waters Show*, a one-off variety show on which Waters sang and performed a scene from the Broadway play *Mamba's Daughters*, in which she was currently performing. For the early part of her career especially, Waters was not the "round" figure of the mammy that both Beavers and McDaniel were. She transitioned into roles that were more mammy-like with her performance in the film *Pinky* in 1949. But no doubt because of her deep understanding of the problems of stereotypes, her Dicey was not the typical mammy. As Bogle says of this performance, "though the part was written with the characteristics of the traditional self-sacrificing mammy, she nonetheless distinguished her Dicey with a warmth and humanity that transformed the character and transcended the stereotype itself" (2011, 438). Here, we see what is ostensibly a character of the white imaginary transformed in the hands of an experienced actor into something deeper than the stereotype. This is one of the primary negotiations that Black women actors of this period made; their desire to act, combined with their skill and their political awareness, led them to create roles that on the surface appear to replicate negative stereotypes, but when examined more deeply, reveal a more three-dimensional picture of Black life.

Her long career led Waters to her most notable stage role, that of Berenice in *Member of the Wedding* (1950) (which would also lead to her being in the film, as well). With her vast experience on the stage, Waters could do a bit of picking and choosing, and she initially refused to do the role of Berenice (Bogle 2011; Regester 2010). As Waters noted in her autobiography, "Free to give my own interpretation, the character of Berenice satisfied me. She had been buffeted plenty, but now she was not without humor, and she had retained her faith in God" (quoted in Regester, 248–9). To an even greater extent than McDaniel in *Gone with the Wind*, Waters's stature in the field enabled her to modify a role to one that better reflected the lives of Black women on the screen. Her time on *Beulah* would not permit her the same kinds of latitude, as we will see.

Hattie McDaniel

Hattie McDaniel, in part because of her Academy Award for her role as "Mammy" in *Gone with the Wind*, has long been deeply associated with the mammy role. Her screen roles were usually, if not always, criticized by the Black press of the time, even while some viewers appreciated that she made attempts to increase diversity in Hollywood. So much of her reputation is based on her work in *Gone with the Wind* that the film deserves some attention. But it is also important to understand McDaniel in a larger context, that of her career over the long term and how she approached acting. My focus on this aspect—acting and the craft of acting—is important because I believe it accounts for some of the differences I will discuss later in my analysis of *Beulah*.

McDaniel came from a performing family, of sorts. Her father was a Civil War veteran who moved his family from the South to Denver, Colorado. McDaniel watched her father's long struggle for veteran's benefits after he was severely injured during the war, and this struggle made her acutely aware of systemic racism in ways that others might not have seen. She grew up in an integrated city that had a significant Black population. And she began her career on the stage, working with her siblings (particularly her brother) in vaudeville. McDaniel developed her craft on the stage, and this skill—playing to live audiences—requires a different type of training and acting skill that, while it transitions well to the screen, is not the same. There are no multiple takes on stage, no editing; stage actors develop and hone skill that those who begin in film or television do not necessarily develop.

In addition to the skill in acting, McDaniel's history of working in vaudeville gave her a perspective on performance that Beavers would never have to develop. Her siblings challenged the performance of the time; her brother Otis actually developed a whiteface act, that, as Jill Watts explains, was something that in many parts of the country might have gotten him lynched (2005, 35). Back in Denver, Hattie performed in vaudeville and in Blackface minstrelsy. Particularly when Black-in-Blackface minstrelsy was performed for Black audiences, it was understood to be at least in part "signifyin'" on white-in-Blackface minstrelsy (Anderson 1995).[3] Watts's biography of McDaniel argues this point strongly: "Although on the surface McDaniel-Hickman's image reinforced the most horrific racist stereotypes of black women, her audience clearly understood her intentions. The popular entertainer was parodying the foolish, silly, and asexual caretaker Mammy. [...] she exaggerated her curves to create a character that was not passive and acquiescent but rather assertive and bold" (Watts 2005, 40–1).

McDaniel, therefore, was aware of the negative stereotype of the mammy and sought to subvert it. This type of performance continued as she shifted from the stage to the screen. She auditioned for the role that Beavers won in *Imitation of Life* but was not hired in part because her portrayal was too assertive. Where Beavers was the very type of mammy character the producers wanted, McDaniel was not.

When *Gone with the Wind* went into production in 1938, the plan was to create an epic film based on Margaret Mitchell's novel of the same name. But as David O. Selznick began to cast the film, he was surprised to encounter resistance to the novel and script as it was written. Butterfly McQueen auditioned for the film without knowing that the role for which she was auditioning was a slave (Hinton 1988). One might argue that had the actors read the novel, they would have known what the film was, and the roles for which they were auditioning. In spite of that, this was an opportunity in an industry and a time in which roles for Black actors, male and female, were heavily proscribed as specific stereotypes (Bogle 1996). I think it's important to consider the context of the time and to read the film, perhaps, oppositionally, which might lead us to reconsider how McDaniel and her coactor Butterfly McQueen have historically been viewed. I will argue here that several factors led to changes that make *Gone with the Wind* fundamentally different in its depiction of Blacks, especially Black women, particularly when compared to other films of the same era. This is important because it goes to the root of who McDaniel was and how she approached her roles in film and *Beulah*. As Miriam Petty argues, McDaniel "attempt(ed) to reimagine the character along ideological lines that reflected notions of respectability as articulated by African American church- and clubwomen who wanted to claim autonomy over their own lives and public images" (2016, 29).

I have watched *Gone with the Wind* many, many times. When I wrote about McDaniel and Mammy while working on my dissertation and in my first book, what I saw was what most people see in the film: a racist caricature of Black womanhood. Since then, I have watched the film in the course of teaching it in the context of film portrayals of women of color, primarily in Hollywood film. And as I watched *Gone with the Wind* next to other films of the period (and slightly earlier, such as *Imitation of Life*), I noticed some stark, and perhaps significant, differences in McDaniel's Mammy.

First, while of course as a slave Mammy was uneducated, she was not unintelligent. As McDaniel played her, she understood the culture in which she lived and was capable of navigating both antebellum and reconstruction cultures while also having abundant knowledge of everyday things (had it not been in part from Mammy's ingenuity, the O'Hara girls might have died after the war). She had knowledge and she used it. McDaniel's characterization of Mammy is deeply humanized. Her portrayal creates screen moments in which Mammy is relatable, such as the scene late in the film when she brings Melanie to the house to attempt to heal the rift between Scarlett and Rhett after Bonnie's death. She also had power within the household. While limited, certainly, it was present and she acted on it (a stark contrast to Beavers's powerless mammies).

When I look at McDaniel's portrayal now, I see an accomplished actor making her way in an industry that would happily have confined her to the stereotype of the mammy. She played mammy with a twist, as it were; yes, she begins the film as a house slave and ends the film as a house servant, but her performance is much more than that. We see her wield what power she has used her intelligence to make sure she (and her "family") survives. Look carefully at McDaniel as she plays the aging Mammy, and you see her efforts to humanize the character by giving her a subtle but clearly visible limp. Moments like these occur throughout the film, and McDaniel's care in constructing the character (scene study) and determination to make Mammy more than just a maid is evident.

What we see here is the skill of the actor as she creates a role that on the surface is only the stereotype that the (white) writers of the film script saw in the original novel. To watch the film cursorily is to miss the skill of McDaniel's performance and the ways that she works to bring deeper dimensionality to the character of Mammy (Anderson 1997). It is this skill that McDaniel translates into *Beulah*, first on radio, then on television.

Louise Beavers

Beavers is unlike either McDaniel or Waters; she did not come to the film industry with a significant career on the stage. Her first role, in a 1929 version of *Uncle Tom's Cabin*, came from catching the attention of a man from central casting who happened to see her in an amateur minstrel group in Los Angeles. Prior to that, Beavers worked as a maid for Leatrice Joy, a silent film actress. Beavers did not seem to have a strong sense of connection to a tradition of Black performance, and her context was the roles she saw in early film while she worked for Joy. For the most part, her reputation was of someone who was willing, without too much pushback, to play the subservient, white-imagined roles for Black women in Hollywood. As Charlene Regester notes, Beavers "contended that she resisted [taking a film role] 'because of the African roles given to colored people'" (2010, 73). Her threshold for what was offensive was, therefore, fairly low; any role that was not an "African savage" was not a problem. Indeed, "as an actress and as a person, Beavers provided the vehicle by which Hollywood could experiment with Blackness" (79). Unfortunately, most of that experimentation involved creating characters out of a white imaginary that could not conceive of Black people, let alone Black women, as fully human. This will remain an issue for television writers and producers until the end of the twentieth century and beyond.

Beavers's role as Delilah in *Imitation of Life* is classic, frequently cited as a prime example of the "mammy." While Delilah is noted for her compassionate if misguided care for her daughter Peola (played by Fredi Washington), she is very much the epitome of the ignorant Black mammy. She only ends up at the house of her future employer because she misread the job advertisement in the paper; when offered a share of the profits from the pancake mix that is her secret recipe, she refuses, asserting that she just wants to be a maid.

Beavers's Delilah is very much the image of the Black maid in the white imagination; in other words, the character that Beavers performs conforms to the notion of who and what Black women are in the eyes of whites in the 1930s and 1940s: ignorant, compassionate, and useful. Here, I am using "ignorant" very specifically, because I believe it adequately captures the aspect of the classic "mammy" stereotype. The mammy is not a character who has *wisdom*, even. We can see in the characters that Beavers portrays that these mammies don't only lack formal education—we think education might be wasted on them altogether. This is an essential part of Beavers's mammy portrayal and a key contrast to how McDaniel performs her "mammy." In *Imitation of Life*, Beavers's Delilah might have been in a kind of advisory role to her own daughter, and to Miss Bea and Jessie (Bea's teenage daughter), but she never provides any. There are opportunities for her to impart some wisdom gleaned from her own life experience, but we as audience come to understand that she is not intelligent enough to have the kind of self-awareness that would generate wise advice.

Beavers did not object to any of the elements of the character of Delilah that many find offensive. Delilah cannot see why light-skinned Peola tries to pass at school; and while this is not a value judgment about whether Peola passes or not, Delilah's dogged refusal to see how much her intelligent daughter does not want to be limited by her race is not only a mother's refusal to let go of her daughter but an ignorance about the opportunities that might have been open to Peola.

Delilah's understanding of what might be a "good life" for Peola is limited to being a "good Negro," maybe being a schoolteacher down South, but nothing more—despite the veritable fortune they might have amassed had Delilah not foregone the equal share of the profits from the pancake business. Shrewd Black businesswomen of the 1920s and 1930s would not have given up a share in a business to just be a maid; we have the obvious example of Madame C. J. Walker, who amassed a fortune through her hair and beauty products business and left it to her daughter, A'Leia, who would become a patron of Black artists during the Harlem Renaissance. With this real-life example of Black business success, the image of Beavers as Aunt Delilah, making pancakes and rubbing Miss Bea's feet, reveals the strong influence of the white imaginary over the stories that Hollywood film told.

Beavers is successful in Hollywood because she is willing to play this particular stereotyped role. She can artfully portray the stereotype, evoking that image of Black womanhood so deeply ingrained in the white imagination. Beavers had a bit of trouble with *Imitation of Life*, when she complained about a scene in which Peola calls herself a "nigger" (Regester 2010). Her objection led to the scene being cut. Beavers's history with *Imitation of Life*, and the myriad other films in which she played essentially the same character, set her up to fill the role that Waters and McDaniel had created; but perhaps, as we shall entertain later, her long experience embodying a kind of subservience for white audiences created a bit of a rocky transition into the role of Beulah.

Beulah: The Radio Program (1949–53)

Before we dive more deeply into the television show, we must look at the radio show from which the television show emerged.[4]

In the television version of *The Beulah Show*, the differences between the three different Beulahs are subtle but profound, and I will address those in the next section. But we should start with McDaniel's recreation of Beulah for CBS Radio before delving into the ABC television episodes. Because there are scripts from the radio program, we can examine them to see how McDaniel's work on the radio program (along with her brother, Sam) shifted the representation of Beulah. Working scripts that belonged to Hattie are housed with their papers in the Margaret Herrick Library. The scripts, notations, and edits, as well as episodes of the program available online (prior to McDaniel's casting) and other materials (including interviews and letters) illuminated the radio program and revealed McDaniel's work on the show.

The original radio show *Beulah* was like other radio programs that allegedly portrayed Black life, such as *Amos 'N' Andy*. These programs were just a version of the white-in-Blackface minstrel show in a new medium, with white men playing all characters (including Beulah). They imagined Black life through the eyes of white employers, with no real insight into what the lived experiences of Black people actually were. They spoke in the white imitation of Black dialect, little modified from the minstrel-show days. Black audiences also listened to the programs, understanding them to be poor imitations of Black life. So when Marlin Hurt, who first played Beulah on the radio program, died, CBS and Proctor and Gamble looked to replace him. McDaniel auditioned and was hired in 1947 (Watts 2005). In addition, CBS hired new writers; one of them, Hal Kanter, had worked on *Amos 'N' Andy* and would go on to create and produce *Julia*.

Because of her experience and her politics, McDaniel felt that the program was a place where she could shift representation. After her Oscar win, she gave a speech to a group of Black women in which she said, in part:

> [Playing "Mammy" was] an opportunity to glorify Negro womanhood—not the modern, stream-lined type of Negro woman who attends teas and concerts in ermine and mink—but the type of Negro of the period which gave us Harriet Tubman, Sojourner Truth, and Charity Still. The brave, efficient, hardworking type of womanhood which has built a race, mothered our Booker T. Washington, George W. Carver, Robert Moton, and Mary McLeod Bethune. So, you see, the mothers of that era must have had something in them to produce men and women of such caliber.
>
> (McDaniel, quoted in Petty 2016, 58)

McDaniel did in fact shift *The Beulah Show*. Where the program had previously focused on Beulah's attempts to get her boyfriend, Bill, to propose to her, McDaniel saw an opportunity to make Beulah into a more complex character. McDaniel refused to use dialect and "transformed Beulah into a wisecracking, all-knowing character who was much more sensible and intelligent than the Hendersons, the family she served" (Watts 2005, 255). McDaniel's Beulah was not the same Beulah that listeners had come to know, but they embraced her all the same. The show became very popular, and the addition of McDaniel meant that sponsors had a Beulah they could use visually, particularly in advertising.

McDaniel was accustomed to using the visual to create and "signify" on the stereotyped characters, but that required physical presence; she could not do this on the radio. She felt an overhaul of the program was in order. The Beulah that McDaniel created on the radio was distanced from the radio-minstrelsy of the white actors who had played her. McDaniel's cachet also convinced the show's producers to hire Ruby Berkley Goodwin, a Black actor and writer, to write some of the show's scripts (Watts 2005).

If we just consider what McDaniel's presence could do in a significant revision of the radio show *Beulah*, then we can begin to see the difference that an influential Black presence can have, particularly in the ways that "count." By "count," I mean that they can make some changes in the core of the program that directly counter the stereotypes. They can wield influence that can shift the way people in the industry come to think about and better understand the lives of the marginalized "other," about whom they have scarcely thought, and whose lives they cannot truly imagine. McDaniel insisted that the "new" Beulah no longer speak in dialect (Watts 2005). Instead of being ignorant, she is savvy and more knowledgeable than the whites for whom she works. The addition of a writer whose own experience was closer to that of the character was essential for generating scripts that were closer to the actual lives of Black people. This does not mean that the show completely cast off all stereotypes; after all, Black critical reviews of the show remained poor (often because Beulah, for all her savvy, was still "just a maid").[5] CBS was willing to let McDaniel dictate these important changes, which is attributable to her popularity and the cachet she held within the industry. An examination of some of the scripts, beginning in 1948 (a year after McDaniel joined the show) and concluding in 1950, shows some of the effects of McDaniel's work with the show. We begin with a few early episodes, then move on to consider some of the programs in which McDaniel's influence is visible.

Episode 78: March 10, 1948. Writers: Hal Kanter, Howard Leeds, and Arthur Julian and *Episode 79: March 11, 1948. Writers: none noted on script, but likely Kanter et al.*

These two episodes focus on Beulah getting Bill to marry her. They are early in McDaniel's tenure at the radio show and demonstrate one of the elements that McDaniel sought to change. First, McDaniel wanted to move the show away from its strong focus on the romance between Beulah and Bill. The script features several interesting references, primarily to Shakespeare plays. Beulah says of herself, "my name oughtta be Portia … I'm havin' so much trouble facin' life!" (3). In a section that was cut, Beulah and Oriole discuss various perfumes, trying to find one that will help Beulah be attractive to a secret "ardent admirer" she hopes will make Bill jealous enough to propose.[6] The fragrances are named for classical love pairs—Antony and Cleopatra, Romeo and Juliet … and for comic relief, one called Abbott and Costello. Beulah with McDaniel's influence does say fewer absurdly comic lines, and few to no malapropisms (malapropisms were a staple of the minstrel show). Sherman, Beulah's "ardent admirer," happens to be someone she knew from high school. He seems to be moderately successful and claims that he won't be complete without her. He quickly proposes, and Beulah toys with accepting his proposal. Of the four or so scenes that make up the episode, two of them highlight Beulah's interior life, that is, her life outside of work for the Hendersons (Kanter, Leeds, and Julian 1948). This is a slight improvement over the show before McDaniel, in which scenes that show Beulah's interior life were less present.

In the next episode, we continue with Beulah's dilemma about Sherman's proposal, while her "heart still belongs to Bill" (3). Alice Henderson thinks that Sherman's attention will help Beulah land her desired Bill. Beulah says, "I'm gonna try settin' my cap for Bill … and if that don't work, I'm gonna use Sherman Herman an' try settin' a trap for him!" (5). With McDaniel in the role, jokes about her figure play differently than they might have and strike a poignant note. In comments to herself about her new dress, Beulah says, "It makes your figure look like a schoolgirl's … (CHUCKLES) … Who're you kiddin' Beulah? No matter what dress you wear, your figure looks more like a school <u>house</u>" (5). Beulah's new beau visits while the Hendersons are out. The second scene reveals Sherman's idea of a good wife:

> S: Why you'd be wonderful around the house. You'd cook and wash … and
>   clean … and bake … and dust … and sew … and you could raise a family, too.
> B: Sherman, when would I have time!??
> S: My dear, if you'll accept my proposal of marriage, I promise you that your
>   troubles will be over. (7)

Bill enters, and the two of them get into a bit of a "fight," mostly a verbal confrontation featuring something approximating the "dozens":[7] "I got a mind to hit this runt so hard, his ears'll resign from his head" and "You get outta here or I'll knock your eyes so far back in your head, you'll see where you've been instead of where you're goin'" (9). This sets up an interesting conflict, especially in a program ostensibly designed for white audiences at this particular time. Bill is working class, not highly educated, and largely not financially "successful"; he's ordinary in the way that Beulah is ordinary, which is part of what makes them "work" in the popular imagination as a couple. Sherman, however, is presented as a successful businessman who doesn't quite promise Beulah a life of luxury (far from it) but can afford his expensive tastes in clothing and entertainment (he takes her out for a night of dinner and dancing at the Cuban Club). His language is devoid of any dialect markers. In essence, then, *The Beulah Show* is showing class and educational diversity among Blacks. And despite Sherman's wooing, Beulah seems bound and determined to only use Sherman's attention as a way to make Bill jealous.

Episode 103, Wednesday, April 14, 1948. Writers: Arthur Phillips, Chuck Stewart

This episode, which comes a bit more than a year into McDaniel's tenure on the radio program, is one of the richest, for our purposes. Specifically, this script reveals some of the kinds of changes McDaniel commented that she wanted to make to the show ("an opportunity to glorify Negro womanhood" (Regester 2010, 148)). Beulah's sense of obligation to family and to smoothing the future path of the next generation emerges here as important to Beulah (and was in line with McDaniel's politics). Beulah and Bill seem settled after their near-breakup in March. Beulah's third cousin, Vivian, has come to visit and is staying with Beulah. In the first scene, Bill arrives to enjoy some breakfast with Beulah. When she tells him that Vivian is not yet up, he suggests that sleeping in will make it difficult for Vivian to get a job as a housekeeper. Beulah's reply is startling, for a late 1940s audience:

> Vivian ain't gonna be no housekeeper. I mean, I'm going to see that she gets advantages. She's going to have all the things I didn't have when I was a girl. […] I've made up my mind, Bill. Vivian is going to get an education. […] I want her to get smart brains …. Read interesting books, like the Encyclopedia Britannica.
>
> (5)

Obviously, the encyclopedia comment is for laughs, but Beulah's desire for her cousin is profound and challenging at a time pre-*Brown v. Board*. Even more poignant is a line that was cut: "I want Vivian to know all about painting and sculpture. When she sees a painting she should know right away who painted it. And when she seems some sculpture, she should know who scalped it" (5). And while this notion of educated Black people is progressive, we don't expect that it will be too much; Vivian isn't going to be a doctor or lawyer. As Beulah says, "I want her to become a professional woman. [...] Like maybe a school teacher ... or a dental assistant." So the possibilities are not endless, but Beulah is strongly advocating for her cousin to *not* be a domestic. A school teacher was a significant opportunity open to Black women during this period and situates the *moment* as one that reflects a knowledge or understanding about opportunities for young Black women outside of being a domestic, and simultaneously the veneration with which teachers were held in Black communities.

But because this is a comedy, and there must be some conflict that will generate laughs, Beulah quickly realizes that college is expensive and that Vivian will have to get a job to help pay for the tuition. Vivian, who is played by Butterfly McQueen, is clearly not cut out for more advanced study; she tries unsuccessfully to get a job in a drug store. While Beulah's (and McDaniel's) efforts are not successful, the idea of college-educated Black people enters into the world of the radio show. This episode very much aligns with McDaniel's political and philosophical perspective. Beulah, working hard at her job as a domestic, sacrifices for the next generation, who should be able to take advantage of more opportunities.

Episode 224: Thursday, November 18, 1948. Writers: Hal Kanter, Arthur Julian, and Howard Leeds

Even when the show returned to some of its plot mainstays (in this case, the almost-but-never-actually-happens marriage between Beulah and Bill), incorporating some middle-class sensibilities constitutes another shift. McDaniel was not opposed to the romance plot, as long as the show took up other issues as well. In this episode, we return to the marriage plot. This time, Bill has signed up to take a job in Alaska for a year, and Beulah's response is to either get him to marry her or to not move to Alaska. Bill requests Beulah come to his shop, dressed up; the audience and Beulah think this might be it! Of course, it isn't. In order to go to Alaska, Bill needs to sell his shop, and hopes that he and Beulah, dressed to the nines, will get him a better price. Unfortunately, the person who comes to the shop only wants Bill's tux back. Two of the significant elements of this episode are the notion of well-to-do Blacks: people who are not just middle class but, as evidenced by Bill trying to get Beulah to help him pick out a new yacht, a seriously moneyed class. Did white audiences think such things impossible and nonsensical? Perhaps. But Black audiences knew of other possibilities; within Black communities, there was knowledge of those "exceptional" Blacks who were rich. The other significant element of this episode is that the Hendersons are only minimally present. Instead, this episode gives us a deeper glimpse into the interior lives of Bill and Beulah, and takes us out of imagining Beulah's life as tied, even as an employee, to the Hendersons. When Black life is conceptualized as existing outside of white worlds, it has the effect of seeing Black people as also existing outside of whiteness and the white imaginary.

The final three episode scripts are all from the 1950s, close to but still predating the premiere of the television program in October 1950.

Episode 489: Thursday, January 12, 1950. Writers: Sherwood Schwartz, Arthur Julian, and Howard Leeds[8]

Like so many of the episodes of this daily radio program, there remains a tension between the predominant white imaginary and the little ways that McDaniel and others (actors as well as writer Goodwin) influenced the writers to imagine Black people differently. Episode 489 returns us to some of the familiar strictures on Black possibility that are belied by other episodes. This episode concerns a lawsuit Beulah is considering bringing against the next-door neighbors (the Perrins) because of their sidewalk. She is worried about harm it could cause to Oriole, who works for them. Harry Henderson encourages the suit, prepared to find Oriole another job if she should be fired. For her part, Beulah considers hiring legal representation suggested by Bill, a Mr. Judson, who is not a lawyer but a "Supreme Legal Advisor and Special Consultant on Matters of All Kinds, Inc." So while there were plenty of Black lawyers at the time (Thurgood Marshall would shortly bring a case before the Supreme Court, in fact), Mr. Judson is no great legal mind and is so incompetent he makes Beulah believe she could be jailed for bringing the suit. This kind of depiction of a "separate and not quite equal" Black world reflects the dominant culture understanding (and the white imaginary) of the writers, with a focus on Black incompetence. In this, this episode uses some of the tropes that were a staple in *Amos 'N' Andy*.

Like other Black performance that existed within a predominantly white industry, with a predominantly white audience, *The Beulah Show* portrayed the quotidian concerns of a Black live-in maid during the 1940s and 1950s in ways that often reinforced ideas about who Black people were and what their roles were in white society. But it also had its moments of resistance once Black people became involved in the production. These are often little things; a program from June 27, 1950 (just prior to the show's moving to television) has Beulah and Oriole shopping in a department store with white sales clerks. This is a sharp contrast to the portrayals in episode 489 and aligns with a more progressive political stand like McDaniel's. This moment flies in the face of the ubiquitous segregation that existed in much of the United States in 1950 and imagines a world where a housemaid would be courteously served by a white sales clerk at a large department store. McDaniel's hiring by CBS in 1947 opened the door for other Black performers (including Sam McDaniel) to be hired for other roles. The show's moments of both racial "transcendence" and progressivism (educated and middle-class Black people who were not the stereotype) show us that even with her limited power (McDaniel was not a writer, director, or producer), McDaniel could create subtle shifts in the radio representation of Beulah.

In many ways, I see in this radio show with McDaniel as the "star" many of the same tensions and challenges that were present for Black Blackface minstrel performers during the late nineteenth and early twentieth century. In order to keep their audiences, Black minstrel performers compromised by keeping some of the "classic" minstrel elements even while introducing new and relatively progressive content. *Beulah* on the radio does many of the same things. Episodes that reveal an interior life of Beulah and her community as "respectable" sit uncomfortably next to episodes that show an inherently inferior Black world whose denizens perform menial labor for the "superior" white world. McDaniel's history of pushing representations of Black womanhood, and her persistent desire to reflect the "respectable" Black womanhood of her community, stands out amid scripts that conform to the dominant culture's view of Blackness, Black communities, and Black womanhood. It took McDaniel *actively* engaging with the writers of the program to make these kinds of changes, and ultimately, they constituted only a small percentage of the programming. As Watts notes, "McDaniel immediately took an adamant stand. If she were to play the part, then it would be without Hollywood's contrived and humiliating Black dialect. […] In an attempt to counter *Beulah's* tremendous failings, McDaniel, for one of the first times, flexed some star muscle and immediately set out to overhaul the show" (Watts 2005, 254). When the program moves to television, these kinds of changes will become significantly more difficult.

Beulah Goes to Television

When the decision was made to bring *Beulah* to television, it was on a different network and filmed in New York rather than California, which perhaps explains why Ethel Waters was hired to play the role that McDaniel had, by this point, well established on the radio. I cannot help but wonder how the television show's history might have been different if McDaniel had made the transition to the screen at the beginning of the program, rather than later. At the time, Waters was fully involved with her role as Berenice on Broadway, and, as Bogle notes, the "schedule was grueling" (2011, 458).

The structure of the program necessarily shifts when the program moves from radio (aural) to television (visual and aural). One of the differences that is notable (considering the very few episodes of the program that are readily available) is that the show becomes more focused on the Hendersons and set at the Hendersons's home. On the radio, Beulah can easily move from one location to another, which meant that the audience experiences Beulah in *Black* spaces (from the lodge and clubs to Black businesses). Once the program starts on television, the primary set is the Hendersons's home, and only a few scenes would be shot in other places, even as they might be mentioned. It also means that in spite of its apparent focus on the titular maid, the lives of the Hendersons figured more prominently, perhaps to ease white audiences' relationship to the show.

When it began, *Beulah* was shot in New York, which meant that Waters spent every weekday evening and Wednesday afternoon performing in *Member of the Wedding* and every weekday from 8:30 am to 5:30 pm shooting *Beulah*. Such a schedule took its toll, and the episode of *Beulah* with Waters that I was able to view shows an actor who seems somewhat disengaged and distant from the role. In addition, the show seems significantly more focused on the Hendersons than episodes of the radio show. While the radio show features Beulah in every scene, this episode only features Beulah in about half of the program.

We first encounter Beulah in the kitchen knitting a sweater. She is interrupted by Oriole, played by Butterfly McQueen. Oriole is silly, flighty, with a high squeaky voice, and is focused on getting the ice man to like her. We soon realize that while Oriole is flighty—she can't remember to turn off the water or put the lid back on the cookie jar—she is quite crafty, looking for a way to make Mr. Sprague (the ice man) jealous. She interrupts Beulah's knitting with a visit. In this first scene, Beulah begins, "knit four, purl four, drop two. (Oriole off, high pitch) Here's where I drop everything."

The exchanges (this first scene and the last scene) between Beulah and Oriole are designed, I think, to give the audience a glimpse into Beulah's interior life. While she is ostensibly working for the Hendersons (the episodes imply that Beulah is a live-in maid, rather than someone who comes in daily), she takes time out of her day to do things for herself. We see that Beulah has little patience for Oriole's silliness, expressed through both the dialogue and Waters's body language and facial expressions. She seems tired of Oriole and, perhaps, the stereotype that Oriole plays. She visibly softens when Mrs. Henderson enters the room and engages more positively with her employer than her "friend." She smiles at Alice Henderson's scheme to get her husband to take her out for dinner. This element of the episode is striking, and its subtle formation of an alliance between Alice and Beulah seems to emphasize a kind of camaraderie between a white woman employer and Black servant that belies the history of these relationships (Dill 1994). Waters's presence is calm and authoritative, without signs of obvious subservience or deference to her white employers. Her even vocal tone and lack of a stereotypical "Black" dialect establish Beulah as a different kind of maid than was standard fare in the movies.

This alleged alliance between the women creates an interesting tension in the show, which I might attribute to the subtle conflict between Waters's feelings about the role and knowledge of Black life, and the writers' imaginary of Black life. On the one hand, Alice seems generous and sympathetic to their live-in maid, whom she is happy to give the night off since none of the family will be home for dinner. On the other hand, Mr. Henderson seems oblivious to Beulah having a life outside of his needs. He dumps his associate's daughter off on Beulah for the evening without consultation (he also makes the dinner arrangements without his wife's knowledge) and without knowing that no one is expected to be home that evening. It's something more than just a male-dominated household (or the imaginary of white masculinity in the 1950s) at work here; there's a subtle expectation that nothing Beulah could have planned could be as important as the business dinner. That Alice says Beulah's plans "are just as important" as their own does not change the Hendersons's plans; they "employ" Beulah's boyfriend, Bill, to take care of little Effie for the hour that Beulah will be gone.

Perhaps in keeping with McDaniel's restructuring of the radio Beulah, Waters's Beulah can generally be seen as at least moderately intelligent. She contrasts rather starkly with the other Black characters. Dooley Wilson's Bill performs some of the stereotypes of Black men, which I think are designed to make him less threatening. Beulah is clearly savvier than he is, and a contemporary audience might wonder why someone as smart as Beulah would bother with someone like Bill at all. Bill's misadventures with Effie, who is a most horrible child, make us sympathetic to his plight.

Beulah's relationship with Bill is another glimpse into her interior life, and a contrast from the traditional "mammy" character who is usually shown as asexual. We know that Beulah participates in her sewing circle, and Bill is a member of a lodge. But at least in this episode, we actually don't see that much of Beulah. While the program is ostensibly about her, she is on screen surprisingly little. In fact, Waters is on screen less than ten minutes of the 25-minute program. In contrast, McDaniel was on screen seventeen of the twenty-four minutes in one of her episodes, and in both episodes featuring McDaniel, she is in nearly every scene. While I think this is at least partially attributable to the fact that Waters was limited in her time on the program due to her responsibilities on Broadway, it is interesting that the titular character has such a minor role.

Waters eventually complained that the schedule was too exhausting, and when she signed on to do the film version of *Member of the Wedding*, there was simply no time left to give to the production of *Beulah*. But in some ways the lack of time was an excuse, for as much as Waters wanted to bring dignity to the role, she had little influence over the production. The showrunners had very clear ideas about who and what they wanted Beulah to be, and Waters was not willing to be that type of character: "According to the Black weekly magazine *Jet,* she had left the 'white folks kitchen comedy role'" (Bogle 2011, 460). Bogle relates that "she could never play it as a crude stereotype. Yet likable as she was, she never committed to the character as she did to Berenice. Basically, she kept everything on the surface without any signs of anger or discontent," yet clearly her limits were reached (460).

Production moved from New York to Los Angeles after Waters quit the program after the first season, and ABC could finally hire McDaniel, who lived in Los Angeles, for the television role.[9] McDaniel's long history with the role and her extensive performing career made for a very different Beulah than the one that Waters had portrayed. McDaniel's Beulah bears some resemblance to her *Gone with the Wind* character Mammy; while she does occasionally get into comic situations that are stereotype-derived, she frequently is a dispenser of common sense and everyday wisdom (Figure 1). In the McDaniel episode "Beulah Goes Gardening" (s3:e4, August 12, 1952), the Hendersons try to save money by firing the gardener; if each of the Hendersons pitches in and does some of the work, it will get done. Of course, they all ask Beulah to do their work

Figure 1 Hattie McDaniel as Beulah.

for them. At one point, she insists that she won't serve "her" family cold cuts on a Saturday night—she invokes it as the kind of promise bound to be broken when she has too much work to do. In addition to the gardening, she gets into a problem when she digs up the prize, but ailing, rosebush and takes it to the nursery for a diagnosis. The nursery sells the rosebush to someone else, who does not want to return it. There is a lovely physical comical scene where she runs around with the lawn mower, and another where she tries to trim the hedge evenly and it winds up being only a few inches tall by the time it's even. After a long Saturday of yardwork, she passive-aggressively says to the Hendersons about dinner: "It's burned but don't blame me, it was prepared by a field hand, not a cook." But it's fairly clear from the beginning that Beulah saw the writing on the wall (that the Hendersons would all ask her to do their share of the gardening). She uses the glitches (including the rosebush incident) to teach the Hendersons a lesson, much the way that Mammy might have in *Gone with the Wind*. The episode ends with the Hendersons rehiring the gardener after Beulah pretends to give them cold cuts for dinner on a Saturday night.

Another television episode with McDaniel as Beulah is more focused on the family than Beulah, although she still is in most of the scenes. This time, the episode focuses on Donny, who is having trouble in his dance class, much to his parents' chagrin. When his assigned date stands him up, Beulah tries to get him a new date, with Oriole's help. Little does Beulah (or the Hendersons) know, the "little girl" of the family who recently moved to town is actually a teenager. Beulah and Bill can't teach Donny how to waltz but do teach him how to jitterbug. The dance doesn't end well, but Donny isn't the failure with girls that his mother feared; in fact, after he showed off his jitterbug moves at the dance, the girls are all begging for dance lessons from him. Like many sitcoms, the comedy comes in the form of the initial misunderstanding (courtesy of Oriole, who is well established as not very smart and now played by Ruby Dandridge). In spite of Beulah being "responsible" for both Donny's date and his knowledge of jitterbug, at no point in the episode does Beulah look incompetent or unintelligent; she makes the best choice based on the information she has (although any information from Oriole should always be suspect). And as is typical in the sitcom formula, all is well at the end.

We turn now to the episodes with Beavers. I focus on these last for several reasons. One is simply chronological; Beavers is the last person hired to play Beulah on television, so these are some of the last episodes recorded (even if they were aired out of recording order). I am also interested in seeing how the casting of Beavers in the role of Beulah might have hastened its cancellation. Beavers's lack of experience in theatre and vaudeville made her significantly less aware of the harmful nature of the mammy stereotype, and her work in film, in which actors have far less say in making changes to characters, was also part of her lack of assertive influence when it came to *Beulah*. By the time the episodes with McDaniel aired, the NAACP was already targeting the show with a letter-writing campaign. While any number of factors may have led to the network's decision to cancel *Beulah*, it might have had a resurgence in popularity once McDaniel took over the role (critics had complained about Waters's "stiffness" and visible discomfort with acting on the show, where McDaniel's performance, what remains of it, carries with it the wink and nod of the Black vaudeville performers, and retains her assertive presence). But Beavers's performance—not much distant from the submissive, ignorant mammy she'd been playing since the 1930s—could only have heightened the growing opposition to the program.

Both of the episodes with Beavers focus not on Beulah but primarily on the Hendersons, either on Donny or Alice and Harry as a couple. Beulah's ability to misunderstand things is heightened; in this, these two episodes seem much further away from the first season episode, in which there's no foolish misunderstanding by Beulah at all, or the final McDaniel episode (gardening) which is strongly focused on Beulah. Aside from mentions of the communication among the servant class, there doesn't seem to be much interior life for the Black characters of *The Beulah Show*, which is a significant departure from the radio show, which, especially during the McDaniel years, prominently featured the lives of Beulah and Bill outside of Beulah's work for the Hendersons. Both of the Beavers episodes rely on Beulah's penchant for misunderstanding just about everything and making drastic (incorrect) conclusions. This is a stark difference between the characters as she was played by Waters and McDaniel, as those Beulahs were portrayed as at least savvy, if not intelligent. While this might be attributable to a show nearing its end, having run out of plots and comic situations, the radio program would continue beyond this; the increasing pressure from Black critics and the NAACP found fuel in Beavers's portrayal.

Beulah has an opportunity to ask Alice about the delivery of a baby carriage in "The New Arrival" but never does. Beavers's Beulah not only presumes the carriage's arrival reveals a pregnancy but quickly spreads this misinformation (and it moves like wildfire through the neighborhood once Oriole begins to retell the story to her network). In "Second Wedding," Beulah sees the "danger signs of marriage disintegration" in every action or inaction of the Hendersons and works herself up about it. She spends the rest of the episode trying to fix what wasn't broken (but begins to fracture as a result of her meddling). Beavers has none of McDaniel's assertive presence, and as a result both of the episodes show a Beulah who doesn't even seem to be sufficiently competent to fix the household's problems. Beavers plays Beulah as though she is a competent housekeeper, but is bumbling; she is more deferential to the Hendersons in her manner, if not her dialogue. She speaks more slowly than McDaniel, whose vocal style was short and sharp; this slower way of speaking seems to reflect slower thinking.

The contrast between these episodes and the gardening episode is stark. Where the McDaniel episode has Beulah figure out the solutions to her problems (particularly getting Harry's prize rosebush back), the Beavers episodes have the problems resolved without Beulah; she ends up being a fairly minor figure in "The New Arrival" and more problem than solution in "Second Wedding." She is challenged shutting down Oriole's foolishness. Beavers annoyingly (at least to my ears) sings "Nobody Knows the Trouble I've Seen" with additional improvised lyrics. She seems incapable of solving problems, where McDaniel's Beulah leveraged her knowledge to find solutions. We see Beulah go from being perhaps unlucky but endowed with life wisdom to being unintelligent. Beavers's Beulah strongly recalls her other film mammy work, particularly her role in *Imitation of Life*.

Beavers performed in thirty-three episodes of the program—almost the entire 1952 season. According to Brooks and Marsh, Beavers quit the show at the end of the 1952 season. She did go on to take a role in a film (*Never Wave at a WAC*) in 1953, and would return to television in *The Danny Thomas Show* for six episodes in 1953.

Hollywood "Success" and What It Took

The three women who played Beulah were all "successful" in the world of film, and to a lesser degree, in television (and radio). As a historical marker of a particular time, *The Beulah Show* gives us insight into the late 1940s and early 1950s, and the white imaginary of the period. This program, which emerged as a radio version of Blackface minstrelsy, was somewhat transformed by Hattie McDaniel during her time on it. These changes happened in part because McDaniel, an Academy Award winner, had sufficient influence in Hollywood to apply subtle pressure to the industry (or, at least, these writers and producers) to shift, if not transform, the representation of this particular Black woman on television. What McDaniel brought to the radio show, by her presence and her insistence upon including Black writers and actors, was some representation of Black interior life—Black life as it was lived outside of the homes of white employers. I believe that this was partially because of the respect that McDaniel had for the work done by Black domestic workers, Black women who worked and sacrificed so that their children would have better lives. As noted in her speech after *Gone with the Wind*, she saw the importance of the work of Black women in a way that reflected the ideology of Black clubwomen—both in terms of respectability politics and in terms of "lifting as we climb." Certainly, she was a professional actor, but in her work as an actor, she felt it her responsibility to ease the path for the next generation and for her contemporaries, as well.

There was great potential in *The Beulah Show*, particularly as influenced by McDaniel. She was invested in representing Black people, Black women, in dignified ways. If the white imaginary could not conceive of, or represent, Black people as lawyers, doctors, and teachers, she could at least represent Black working-class folk in ways that challenged the offensive stereotypes that predominated. In a 1947 letter to columnist Hedda Hopper, McDaniel wrote:

> So I do not feel that I have disgraced my race by the roles that I have played. I'll close this issue by saying that I am trying to fathom out in my mind as to just what an Uncle Tom is.[10] People, who can afford it, certainly have maids and butlers. Yet, are these people who work as maids and butlers called Uncle Toms? Truly, a maid or butler in real life is out making an honest dollar, just as we are on the screen. I only hope that the producers will give us Negro actors and actresses more roles, even if there will be those who call us Uncle Toms.
>
> (McDaniel 1947)

We cannot know what changes McDaniel might have brought to the role had she not fallen ill. What is clear is that the hiring of Beavers to replace McDaniel ended the possibility of significant changes to the nature of the character of Beulah, because Beavers's perspective on the politics and aesthetics of the representation of the Black "maid" was not progressive; she did not have the knowledge and the political savvy to consider making *Beulah* a different kind of comedy about Black people. Her acting and her way of performing the mammy character were insufficient to pull off the assertive, competent Beulah that McDaniel was developing.

We are also treated to McDaniel's philosophy surrounding her work in Hollywood and the contention over what kinds of Black people would be represented. McDaniel's point here is that there is dignity in work, even if that work is in a servile role, and to portray dignified Black people (to the extent possible, given the strictures of the white imaginary) who are working class is not necessarily to embody a negative stereotype. If the objection of audience and critics alike is to the representation of Blacks only as working class and in service roles, then one might imagine that a show based on Blacks in different roles might appeal to audiences. If the objection is about *how* the working class is represented, that's a slightly different matter. As stated earlier, the television program is called *The Beulah Show*, but it is really about the Hendersons. Beulah is ostensibly the main character, but the television show shifts focus away from Beulah and toward the Henderson family. I continue to imagine that, with McDaniel's politics, had she not had to leave the show, the representation of Beulah (and the entire program) might have changed.

The reality of "Beulah" and the way the program constructs an image of Black womanhood is threefold. First, while McDaniel is correct about the importance of showing the dignity of Black working people, this representation was one of only a very few. In effect, the ideology perpetuated by *Beulah* was not inconsistent with the larger US postwar ideology, as yet untouched by the emerging Civil Rights movement. Second, Beulah's interior life—what parts of it we see—shows Blacks in a segregated world that only intersects with the white world in the area of work. The fact that Beulah focuses on the white family as "her family," that she never does marry Bill or have children of her own, supports a view of Black life as only ever in service of white people and whiteness. I think that it was not so much that Beulah was a maid that so angered Black audiences, but that she seemed happy to be a maid, with no desire to live the life that Alice Henderson lived (at least on the television version).

Third, it is also clear from the extremely limited views we have of Beulah's interior life that the show's writers had little to no knowledge about what Black people did when they were not working for white people. They had sources under their noses; they had Black actors who could have provided them with significant elements of Black culture that were based on their own lived experiences. They could have asked, or listened to Black actors giving them suggestions about what might make the show more popular with Black audiences. But as Hal Kanter said about his work on *Amos 'N' Andy*:

> I don't think that the sponsor of the network, and certainly not the writers, ever considered the questions of race relations, of stereotyping, et cetera. That was the furthest from our minds. Again, what we were trying to do was to present an amusing set of characters in as amusing a background as we possibly could, doing amusing things to entice that audience to come back next week.
>
> (Riggs 1992)

The demise of *The Beulah Show* was celebrated by those who insisted that the show relied on, and perpetuated, stereotypes of Black people. While the show was ostensibly about Black people, most of the episodes focused on the white family that employed Beulah, and not Beulah herself or her life. There seemed little audience for Black people on television, stereotype or not; with *Beulah* cancelled, *Amos 'N' Andy* would be the only television program to feature Black actors until 1953, when it too was cancelled. For the most part, while the Civil Rights movement gained steam, the contested nature of Black Civil Rights was not visible on the small screen, except on news programs. While some Black actors would still work in television during the decade following the demise of *Beulah*, there would be no programs that featured a Black woman as the main character on a weekly basis until the late 1960s, in a time of significant Civil Rights activism and change.

Julia, the "Black Lady" of 1960s Television

When *Beulah* was cancelled in 1952, television was left without a program headlined by a Black woman. Granted, *Beulah* had only been on television for a little over two years, and during that time, it had struggled against campaigns by the NAACP decrying its stereotyped representations of Black people. It also ended somewhat unceremoniously with Louise Beavers in the starring role, whose stereotyped mammies were largely disliked by Black audiences.

Throughout the 1950s, television was a largely white world. The exceptions to this were *The Nat "King" Cole Show*, a musical variety show that centered on Cole. The network presented Cole as a kind of "model of assimilation," but that kind of assimilation quickly ran afoul of Southern audiences (Brooks and Marsh 2007, 964). "It failed to attract a significant audience, and therefore sponsors were reluctant to underwrite the show" (964). The other major exception was Eddie Anderson's appearance as a regular cast member in *The Jack Benny Show*, which began in 1950 and extended through 1965. His role of Rochester is one that, like Stepin Fetchit earlier, made use of common caricatures of Blackness (and of Black men in particular) yet was played in such a way that Anderson's skill and presentational (rather than embodying) style of acting meant that Rochester, while a butler, was played with a wink and a nod, especially to Black audiences.[1] In 1961, the chair of the FCC chastised the industry for its lack of diversity, which at least put the idea of diversifying television into the consciousness of executives, writers, and directors (Riggs 1992). There was "diversity" in variety shows, since Black performers were sometimes popular enough to gain audience approval.

By 1968, when *Julia* debuted, television had become more established. By 1963, 90 percent of US homes had a television (Riggs 1992). Of the programs the networks offered in 1968, there were many variety and situation comedies and a few dramas (police procedurals such as *Dragnet* and Westerns such as *Daniel Boone* and *Gunsmoke*) (Brooks and Marsh 2007). *Julia* was one of the top ten programs according to the Nielsen ratings in 1968, among a group that was composed primarily of situation comedies, along with a couple of variety shows and a Western.[2] For *Julia*, a sitcom about a Black woman, to be in the top ten of television ratings in its first year, is somewhat remarkable. It certainly demonstrates an audience for a certain type of Black programming; we might align *Julia* with the same types of audiences that watched Nat King Cole and who identified with a kind of exceptional, "respectable," and assimilable Blackness.

There are reasons why, within the world of television, much Black presence has been rooted in the situation comedy. At times, this format dominates the medium; in 1968, sitcoms and variety shows populated much of television, with a few hour-long dramas, police procedurals, and Westerns thrown in. Only six of the top-thirty-rated shows were hour-long dramas. Certainly one reason for the presence of the sitcom featuring Black actors would be the predominance of comedy and variety programming in the period. But Robin Means Coleman offers us another factor in the presence of Blacks in the situation comedy, rather than the drama: "drama houses a verisimilitude that demands African Americans be taken seriously, something comedy has never required. The genre of comedy has lulled Hollywood into a formulaic, comfortable sleep that is not only tried and true, but profitable" (Coleman 1998, 1–2). With the exception of a short-lived, six-episode drama in the late 1990s, there will not be an hour-long drama that is led by, or focuses on, Black people until the twenty-first century. When we look for representation of Black women in leading roles, then, we must continue to examine the half-hour situation comedy. As we will see, the form itself is somewhat limiting, and the economics of television production and the persistent stereotypes of Blacks in the United States will limit the possibilities of any truly radical representation for some time.

I argue here that the character Julia marks the introduction of the "black lady" character to television and popular culture (Thompson 2009). This is a significant departure from any other type of representation of Black women up to this point, particularly in white-generated popular culture, whether film or television. Representation of a Black middle class—or at least middle-class sensibilities—is an important step for a genre that had been wedded to the working-class Black stereotypes of the mammy and sapphire just a decade earlier (Beulah, of course, and Sapphire on *Amos 'N' Andy*).[3] This shift in representation is undoubtedly partially driven by changes in US society during the period from 1952 to 1968—the Civil Rights movement and the presence in the media of Black women like Rosa Parks and Coretta Scott King would enter into the white imaginary to generate some different ideas about who and what Black women could be. And the presence of Black women performers like Ella Fitzgerald; Lena Horne; *Julia*'s star, Diahann Carroll; and *Star Trek*'s Nichelle Nichols would allow white audiences to embrace Black women who were outside of the Hollywood strictures on Black possibilities.

For all that "Julia" represents a previously invisible Black middle class, the *way* that this middle-class Blackness is represented is also a source of contention over the program. The realities of Black middle-class life in the late 1960s were not one of the easy integrations into white communities. In fact, Black middle-class people typically remained in segregated Black communities (even if they lived in a home they owned, rather than a rented apartment). We might think here of "Strivers' Row" in Harlem; it was firmly located within Harlem's Black community, but was populated by people who had substantial financial resources. In other cities where Blacks lived during this period, middle-class enclaves typically remained in segregated areas. By 1968, Blacks had begun to make some headway into white areas, but these are still relatively few, and the type of comfortable integration we see in Julia was uncommon. Another element that is only occasionally seen in the program is a reflection of the long history of middle-class Black women, in particular, engaged in certain kinds of service work to the community. This is a tradition that dates back to the Club Women of the late nineteenth century, specifically to the confederation of Black women's clubs, the National Association of Colored Women's Clubs (NACW), led by Mary Church Terrell. Their motto, "Lifting as we climb," reflected a project of racial uplift and the strong sense of community these Black women felt for Black people as a whole. The character of Julia, embodying most of the ideas of "respectability," is an attempted corrective to the mammy and maid characters that populated the television landscape.

So *Julia* sits at this odd confluence of points. It is the first television sitcom to feature a Black woman who is not a domestic (of course, the only previous Black woman featured in a sitcom was *Beulah*). Aside from performances on variety shows, there is a significant dearth of Black women on television at all; the 1967–8 season only regularly featured Nichelle Nichols in *Star Trek*. It was fairly clear that roles like that of "Rochester" in *The Jack Benny Program* were not the types of roles that Black actors wanted, nor that some Black audiences were interested in watching. *Julia*, then, takes its place as not only the first television representation of Black middle-class, educated women but ostensibly one of the types of roles Black audiences had wanted more than a decade earlier, when they wrote letters protesting *The Beulah Show*. Here, the representation of what W. E. B. Du Bois referred to as the "talented tenth," the educated middle class, allows Black audiences to see a different kind of representation on television. For the young Black woman who lives in a poor or working-class neighborhood, who never otherwise sees Black possibility and futurity, the figure of Julia, as an educated, professional, middle-class Black woman is important. Future generations could come to take these kinds of representations for granted, especially, as we will see, in the 1990s and 2000s.

On the other hand, it is 1968, not 1952, or even 1964. The world outside of the television sitcom is engaged with Civil Rights, the Black Power movement (the 1968 Olympics, for example), the antiwar movement, the feminist movement, and in a year, the Gay Liberation movement—not to mention the assassinations of King and Bobby Kennedy. It is a socially and politically transformative time, as Christine Acham's book *Revolution Televised: Prime Time and the Struggle for Black Power* (2004) so succinctly notes, which puts it at odds with the world of (white) television. In the face of the activism in the "real world," television offers up nostalgia (the Wild West), fantasy, and "law and order." To expect something else from television is to expect something from it that it is not necessarily in a place to give. Television's purpose, throughout its history, has largely been to distract, and marginally to educate. Television likes to be safe. And in spite of its presentation of something "new," *Julia* is "safe."

It also remains true that even with the advent of this new type of Black woman character, and in spite of her relative power in Hollywood, there were still limits to how far the industry could be pushed. While actors have some influence (and famous actors have a little more influence), the people who ultimately make decisions about television programming are the writers, producers, and networks. So we will consider what Carroll and "Julia" *could* do in television, what they did accomplish, and what was left unfinished.

"Part of Who I Am"

Like Ethel Waters, Carroll came to television with a significant stage career behind her. When I argue that the people who take on these original and groundbreaking roles do so in part because they have skills that translate to power in the world of television, I do not do so lightly. It is their skill, and the recognition of that skill in the larger field, that enables them to rely on their own creativity and experience to remake roles in ways that more accurately reflect otherwise invisible segments of Black communities. McDaniel came to the radio program of *The Beulah Show* (arguably the precursor to the television show) with an Academy Award for Best Supporting Actress, the first Black awardee. Diahann Carroll came to *Julia* having been the first Black woman to win a Tony award.

Carroll's early life and career reflect her middle-class Black upbringing and a love of performing, from the church choir to the stage. She grew up in Harlem, where she attended the Music and Art High School, and by the age of fifteen, she was already modeling for *Ebony* magazine. She attended New York University after completing high school. She quickly began singing in night clubs after a 1954 winning appearance on *Chance of a Lifetime*. She quickly moved into a supporting role in the 1954 film *Carmen Jones* and a starring role in the Broadway musical *House of Flowers* (1954). Clearly, Carroll hit the ground running. The fact that she was physically unlike the stereotypical mammy characters (she was tall, thin, and lighter skinned than the women who played the mammy roles) might have meant that she would be pigeonholed in the "sapphire" and "jezebel" roles that typically required hypersexualized Black women (usually with lighter skin). But Carroll's solid middle-class upbringing and her style sense—her short, straightened hairstyle and designer clothing on that model frame—kept her from easily slipping into the stereotypes, if she would even seriously consider performing such roles.

In part because she embodied the idea of the "Black lady," and in part because of her middle-class upbringing, Carroll was glamorous but not sexual. She read for the lead role in *Carmen Jones*, but did not possess the same potential to be sexualized as Dorothy Dandridge, who was cast in the lead role. Being cast in the film also opened her eyes to the fact that the jobs offered to Black actors in Hollywood were always constructions of the white imaginary. Of *Carmen Jones*, Carroll said, "the original melodies were given new lyrics that reflected someone's misbegotten idea of how black people were supposed to speak. The plot and the characters and situations were every bit as stereotyped as the 'dees,' 'dems,' and 'dats' that filled the dialogue" (Carroll and Firestone 1986, 47). Once on the set, Carroll would find that the actors would be the only Black people working on the film, and it quickly became clear to her that the actors were "outsiders" on the set and in Hollywood itself (47). This kind of situation— where a white crew, directors, and producers created something ostensibly about Black life—was standard in Hollywood at the time and would continue to be for decades. In this situation, it was impossible for these films and programs to treat Black life as anything other than alien, outside, and inferior.

One great benefit of doing the role in *Carmen Jones* was it convinced Carroll, who had attended a performing arts high school but who had been focused on voice, to take seriously the project of becoming a trained actor. While she would spend much of her career prior to *Julia* focused on her signing, that work on her acting craft would become valuable in a few short years, when she would study at the Actor's Studio.

Carroll had auditioned for a role in *House of Flowers* toward the end of the filming of *Carmen Jones*. While she had not yet completed her training at the Actor's Studio and was only nineteen, Carroll was surprised to receive her first Tony nomination for her performance in *House of Flowers*. While she wouldn't win this time, the nomination demonstrated Carroll's talent and the recognition she was beginning to receive from producers and directors. She would take small parts when offered, and continued to sing at various clubs when the opportunity arose. While sometimes frustrated with the roles she was offered (she nearly didn't take the part in *Porgy and Bess* because she thought the stereotypes were offensive), Carroll continued to hone her craft and make a name for herself.

In 1962 she starred in the Rodgers and Taylor musical *No Strings* on Broadway. It was Rodgers's first musical after the death of Oscar Hammerstein, and its use of an interracial love plot seems incidental. The musical is lacking in specific references to race, which in 1962 undoubtedly struck some viewers as a glaring omission, but considering Rodgers's oeuvre, should not be surprising. Carroll played a model, Barbara Woodruff, who while living in Paris meets an American writer who is trying to overcome his writers' block by living there. The decision to cast Carroll came to Rodgers after seeing her on *The Tonight Show*. The theme of the star-crossed lovers is a popular one in the musical genre, and the characters' decision to part while the writer returns to his home in Maine speaks indirectly to the challenges of interracial relationships in the United States without ever actually discussing them. Because the musical never explicitly mentions race or the resistance to interracial relationships in the United States, the show ends up seeming "color-blind," a strange note to strike for a play that would be on Broadway a few short years before the *Loving v. Virginia* case would strike down antimiscegenation laws across the United States. The role would win a Tony for Carroll, the first Tony award for a Black woman for Best Actress in a Musical.[4] It would also lead Carroll to the following conclusion:

It struck me that the main problem [in the writing of *No Strings*] would be finding a writer familiar with black people, someone who would be able to write convincingly about the struggles of a young woman who has made her way through the fashion world. When I ventured that opinion, he [Richard Rodgers] remained noncommittal.

(Carroll and Firestone 1986, 108)

These few sentences reflect the thoughts of so many Black actors, across theatre, television, and film, especially in the mid- to late twentieth century. A year after the 1961 FCC statement on diversity, Carroll would testify before Congress "about the limited opportunities afforded to black performers" not long after she was passed over to play the role she developed on Broadway in the film version of *No Strings* (116–17). Carroll was upset to not be cast after the time and effort she had put into developing the character. "But the fact that they didn't select a black actress (Nancy Kwan was Eurasian, a minority, but she was *not* black) told the story. It was explained to me that a black actress was not box office" (116). As long as the people creating the representations of Black people had little contact with and no respect for African American culture, the characters they created across the media would continue to be shallow caricatures of Blackness.

From "Beulah" and "Amos" to "Julia"

During the 1950s Hal Kanter worked as a writer and producer for both radio and television programs. He had been a writer for the radio program of *The Beulah Show*, including some of the scripts discussed in the previous chapter. Kanter's episodes are mostly episodes in which Beulah is still focused on getting Bill to marry her, either earlier or later in the show's run. In other words, none of those scripts have notably progressive material. Kanter was also a writer for *Amos 'N' Andy*. As Yuval Taylor and Jake Austen note, "Describing his motivations for presenting these paragons, and taking responsibility for an earlier gig, *Julia's* producer-writer Hal Kanter explained, "I really owed to my black colleagues some sort of apology for a lot of things we had done on *Amos 'N' Andy*" (Riggs 1992; Taylor and Austen 2012). Kanter, who had grown up in the South (Savannah, Georgia), like most writers of his generation wrote from what he knew. It was likely that Kanter's only exposure to Black life in the segregated South was when Blacks worked for whites. This limited view and understanding of Black life—always and only in relationship with, and tangential to, white life—is a hallmark of the Black characters that come out of the white imaginary (Morrison 1992).

In an interview for the documentary series *Makers*, Diahann Carroll talks about working with Kanter on *Julia*. According to Carroll, Kanter's inspiration for developing *Julia* was his attendance at an NAACP luncheon. While he was certainly exposed to Black actors who were not poor while he worked in Hollywood, it was not really until this luncheon that Kanter was exposed more broadly to the Black middle class. A room full of Black middle- and upper-middle-class people, and speakers who emphasized the importance of integrating Hollywood, inspired Kanter to "make up" for the negative stereotypes in his earlier work with something different. Clearly Kanter's intentions are good, even if he still has a very limited sense of what the Black middle class must be like. His inability to understand or faithfully render a Black middle-class family would eventually doom *Julia* to cancellation.

Carroll first met Kanter while he was casting the show, and she knew that he thought her too elegant for the role. But Carroll impressed him as eminently capable of playing Julia; "she's very close to my upbringing," Carroll explained— "part of who I am." Carroll knew that the role would be controversial; they needed "to be willing to walk away from the clichés and the caricatures of what black people were supposed to be. To re-think those—everybody had to re-think those" (PBS 2013). The character of Julia gave Carroll and Kanter an opportunity to show a different kind of Black woman on television. Some of the challenge lay here; as Carroll said, she had to explain how Julia got where she was, because while "white characters in the middle class who are educated don't need explanation, […] Julia does" (PBS 2013). Carroll's own experience could provide important touchstones for the creation of such a character, but it would require a creative team that was willing to believe in the possibility of a Black middle class and leave some of the creative decisions about creating a life for this character to the person closest to that experience. Unfortunately, while Carroll tried to give the creative team, especially Kanter, information about Black life, he was not always open to hearing her advice. "I began scrutinizing the scripts for blatant examples of racism or just plain ignorance. When I found them, I usually went straight to Hal to discuss them. He always tried his best to hear me, but sometimes we ran into serious problems" (Carroll and Firestone 1986, 148). In an episode where Julia reveals the first time she experienced racism, Carroll thought that the story that Julia tells borders on absurdity—Kanter placed this moment at Julia's high school prom. Carroll responded to Kanter:

> *But where has Julia been?* Until this high school dance she never knew anything at all about racial prejudice? She never experienced it even once? Nobody *ever told her*—not her mother, her father, her sister, her uncle? *Nobody?* There was no television set or newspaper in Julia's young life?
>
> (Carroll and Firestone 1986, 148)

When Carroll discusses the program, she states that for the most part, *Julia* is a sitcom like other sitcoms, with the same general format. Other programs showcased single parents raising children (*Family Affair,* 1966–71), or office/work environments (*Mod Squad,* 1968–73; *Medical Center,* 1969–76); the thing that makes *Julia* stand out from other programs is that its star is a Black woman. This is to say, in a slightly subtler way, that there is not much about the program or the character (at least in Kanter's imagination) that is specifically *Black*. Carroll herself said, "we were very one-dimensional in many areas. She was the perfect mother. What we had to do, I think, was to find a kind of acceptable area that broke down some barriers, and then we were able to move on from there" (Riggs 1992). Yes, there are acknowledgments that Julia is Black in a world in which discrimination is only recently illegal but very much in practice. Kanter's approach is subtle and unlikely to offend (for Southern audiences were easily offended). We can take as an example this telephone exchange, in the pilot episode, between Julia and Dr. Chegley:

> Julia: I'm colored.
> Chegley: What color are you?
> Julia: I'm a Negro.
> Chegley: Have you always been a Negro, or are you just trying to be fashionable? (Carroll and Firestone 1986, 136)

Carroll noticed that while the dialogue and situations in *Julia* did mark progress from the earlier decade of television, from a denial of prejudice to an acknowledgment of both race and prejudice to the point where it was possible to "joke" about them. But Kanter's limited knowledge of Black people and current politics is there, clearly, in the very first episode, when Julia herself uses the term "colored," which in 1968 is already anachronistic. Kanter was surprised to hear that Carroll still experienced discrimination on an everyday basis (as if both the passage of the Civil Rights Act and her success would shield her from racism). Fortunately, *Julia* was well written and had the novelty of the middle-class Black woman (played by the glamorous singer Diahann Carroll), which helped to propel it to early success. Even in that success, though, are the seeds of its demise, and while it was refreshing to see a Black woman on the small screen who was not playing a maid, there were deep flaws in Kanter's understanding of Black middle-class experience, and of Black life in general in the late 1960s, which would result in another letter-writing campaign and another cancelled series. While the show weathered the opposition to it early on, the pressure from that opposition wore on Carroll: "I'm beginning to feel overwhelmed by the pressure. I don't know how much more of it I can take" (149). When Carroll decided she had enough, the show would end.

Episodes of *Julia*: Topics and Moments

Julia was only on television for three years. It was not eligible for syndication the way that so many of the other programs of the time (*Gunsmoke, Adam 12, Get Smart*, etc.) were, since it lacked the requisite number of episodes. In spite of the fact that it was not in syndication through the 1970s and 1980s, it did find an audience on the TV Land network, where it is occasionally shown. But because its broadcast is intermittent, my access to episodes was somewhat limited. I chose fourteen episodes, primarily from seasons two and three. We can see these episodes as largely exemplary, particularly as we see many of the themes that emerge in the early episodes replayed in later episodes (such is the way of the television sitcom). The tension between the potentially transformative content and what ends up merely replicating other (nonblack) television situation comedies reveals the extent to which change is slow to come, even when a show creator ostensibly relies on his "star" to detail the quotidian life that he didn't even know existed (147). Julia works as a nurse at a defense contractor, where she works for a curmudgeonly white doctor (Dr. Chegley) and an equally sharp-tongued white nurse; they are occasionally joined in the office by a security officer. At home, Julia has a son, Corey, and is close friends with her neighbors, the white Waggedorns: Leonard, an LAPD officer; and his wife Marie and young son, Earl; Earl is Corey's best friend and playmate.

There are several themes that emerge in the episodes that are specific to *Julia* (as opposed to other similar sitcoms of the era, like *Family Affair*, which also has a single parent). The foremost of these is the notion of "prejudice" (as opposed to racism) that is present in many of the episodes. In addition to this, episodes take up Julia and her relationship to a larger Black community, Black single mothers (to a degree), Julia as a working mother, and socioeconomic class. We will consider each of these in turn.

Prejudice

Kanter treats prejudice as a personal failing, not as something structural or a core feature of the broader society. We see this in his treatment of incidents of what we would call racism on the show and also in the ways that some other expressions of racism find their way into the show. Also essential to Kanter's view is that *anyone* can be "prejudiced," and there are several episodes in which Kanter ascribes "prejudice" to Black characters. Almost always, it is something that can be overcome by the end of the episode, mostly by people getting to know each other.

In the episode "Paint your Waggedorn" (s1:e10), we are introduced to the Bennetts, an older white couple who live downstairs from Julia and Corey. We learn quite quickly that the Bennetts are not as progressive as the other residents of the apartment building through a series of interactions between the boys, the Bennetts, and their granddaughter. When the boys suggest playing "house," Mrs. Bennett is rather emphatic that her granddaughter Pamela should be "married" to Earl Waggedorn. When crayon drawings show up on the wall inside the apartment building, Mrs. Bennett assumes that it must be Corey who has drawn on the walls. She turns to Mr. Cooper, the landlord, and says to him, "This place is turning into a ghetto," implying in a single statement that Corey is responsible for the drawing and that having Black people in the building is a detriment. At this time redlining is common practice, and even in places outside of the South, segregation in housing is endemic.[5] The integrated Los Angeles apartment building feels both aspirational and fantastical, and only broken up though the addition of the Bennetts. At this point, though, Julia and Corey are the only Black people in the building. Before long, Bennetts, Julia, and Marie are all in the lobby discussing the drawing, but there are no conclusions; Mr. Cooper says he will repaint the wall. In the following scene, Julia talks to Corey about prejudice; she calls Mrs. Bennett a "sad lady." The implication is clearly that "prejudice" (it is never called racism) is a personal failing, not a systemic deprivation of rights. We also learn through this conversation that Pamela now has the crayons, foreshadowing Pamela's eventual discovery as the culprit of the wall drawing. Julia says to Corey, "It's up to us to teach prejudiced people how wrong they are," and that "prejudice is what causes all of the trouble in this world" (Ruskin 1968).

Eventually, the Bennetts's racism is "cured" by a generous act from Julia. We see that Mr. Bennett is not quite as prejudiced as his wife, and when Pamela chokes on something, he immediately goes to Julia's apartment—after all, Julia is a nurse—for help. Julia helps Pamela cough up what she had swallowed—a piece of crayon. By saving Pamela's life, Julia earns an apology from Mrs. Bennett, especially as she reveals the crayon-marked wall in her own apartment; clearly, Pamela was the one who made the original drawing in the hallway, not Corey.

This episode, one-third of the way through *Julia's* initial season, reveals much about how whites have imagined, and continue to imagine, that racism functions. First, there is the notion that until this moment, Julia has never had to explain racism to her young son. The idea that Corey, as a young Black child—a young Black boy—would not have had any experience with prejudice until this moment is a stretch. Black children, especially those in integrated environments like Corey, would by age six or seven (school-age) have heard racial slurs or experienced some discrimination even if they had not recognized it as such.[6] Racism (or, rather, "prejudice") is explained as a personal failing, or ignorance, something that can be "cured" by education, or when a Black person saves your grandchild's life. The swiftness of Mrs. Bennett's reversal after Julia saves Pamela is somewhat absurd; she also never apologizes for blaming Corey for her own granddaughter's vandalism.

There is a similar pedagogical message to "Romeo and Julia" (s2:E9). Here, in an episode that has Julia set up on a blind date with a friend of one of her colleagues at work, the writers address a different kind of prejudice—the prejudice of Black people. There is an implication that this prejudice is just as bad as the prejudice of people like Mrs. Bennett in the first season. Ostensibly, this episode is about playing cupid for Julia, but is actually about equivalence, or providing "evidence" that Black people can be "prejudiced" too (because no one in Julia's world is a racist, only "prejudiced"). At the same time, we see Julia combating her own suspicions of white people while trying to live an antiprejudiced life.

Mr. Barnes sets Julia up on a blind date with a friend of his, Jordan Hayes. She somewhat reluctantly agrees. When we meet Jordan, we are quickly led to understand that he doesn't like white people. He comments that her apartment building's "color scheme" has "too much white." Julia goes out with him anyway. While she insists that "people are individuals like you and me," Jordan details some of the history of racial discrimination particular to Los Angeles for her to explain why he feels the way he does. Her conclusion? "Jordan Hayes, you are prejudiced." She explains to him that she is "prejudiced against prejudice." Their date ends pleasantly enough, but the planned nightcap is a drink with the Waggedorns, and Leonard Waggedorn is a Los Angeles police officer. Julia and Marie are concerned about how things will go, especially as they leave the two men alone together.

Leonard asks Jordan, "What's your beef?" and the two men proceed to have a heated discussion. Lest we worry too much that the two will come to blows over racism, we quickly find that they are arguing loudly not about racism or "prejudice" but a nearly ancient high school football championship game in which they played on opposite teams. There's no worry that they will have a real conversation about the very real problems of racist policing in Los Angeles in the late 1960s (Bultema 2013); after all, this is a sitcom. Jordan and Leonard have a nice conversation, because in the world of the nonoffensive situation comedy, racism can be overcome by a conversation, and anyone can be prejudiced, even Black people.

One of the most serious episodes about racism (or "prejudice") comes in season 3, when it is time for Corey's eighth birthday party ("That New Black Magic," S3:E13). Corey invites his handball friend, Michael, to his party. Michael informs Corey the next day that he will not be able to come to the party. When Corey asks if he has other plans, Michael explains that when he showed his father a picture of Corey in the yearbook, his father tore up the invitation and refused to give him permission to attend the party. Both boys are sad about the turn of events. Julia asks Corey why he's sad, and he explains the circumstances. He tells her that Michael's dad "must be one of those people we've discussed before, who don't like someone because of their color or religion." This is how Julia has explained racism to Corey, and how he understands it. After the party, Corey brings cake (and ice cream, which melts) to Michael, and the two of them become symbolic of a potential future where these things don't matter. Maybe next year, Michael will be able to attend Corey's birthday party. She does at least comment that she has had this discussion with Corey before. In light of the myriad Black parents who tell of having "the talk" with their Black sons, Julia and Corey live in a world in which structural violence against Black boys and men seems strangely absent. And while this series was filmed and took place in the late 1960s, "the talk" is not new.

Unlike other moments of racism in the series, which is usually overcome by the "prejudiced" person having a moment of recognition in which they recognize the person of the other race as human, this episode leaves the problem of Michael's dad unresolved. Of the episodes I watched, this one struck me as the most real. In 1968, there are plenty of whites who share this sentiment with Michael's father—that they do not want their children playing with Black children. I think this moment at the end of the episode, with Corey and Michael representing a "color-blind" future, is at once an appeal to the rhetoric of assimilation (often encapsulated with the excerpted quote from Dr. Martin Luther King Jr. about being judged "not by the color of their skin, but by the content of their character"). This moment is both aspirational, as a place at which we have not yet arrived as a nation, but for a moment was a potential future. This moment is not alone in terms of an appeal to an ideal of racial harmony and equality that seemed to be emergent at the time.

There is one final episode to consider when thinking about how the show deals with prejudice. In this episode (s2:e9) (discussed below for other themes), Corey wants to go to a party with a classmate, who is a white girl. Julia takes him to their very nice house and is somewhat reluctant to leave him because she doesn't know the family. She is also put off by Cindy's mother's praise of Corey's behavior; it is "a little too sincere." Julia's response to this praise strikes me as a moment that might have been generated by Carroll herself, as it does not reflect Kanter's knowledge or understanding; as shown above, Kanter had very little knowledge or awareness of the realities of Black life. Julia is concerned over the potentially unacknowledged prejudice in Cindy's parents, because their praise of Corey presents itself as though Cindy's parents expected Corey to behave differently than he does. In spite of her reservations, she leaves Corey (who ends up having a good time). This moment is not necessarily one of hidden or unacknowledged prejudice, even though it may seem like it at the time. Instead what comes across in Carroll's performance is a worry for her Black son with white people she does not know. This is one of those moments when Carroll presents us with a slightly different mother figure, one who can more readily acknowledge that racism can be anywhere, including with seemingly well-intentioned people.

Julia and Black Los Angeles

Because the series is primarily focused on Julia's interactions in her workspace and at home (which, as we have noted above is only minimally integrated), there are fewer opportunities to see Julia interact with a larger Black community in

Los Angeles. In one episode, Julia insists upon purchasing a new car from a Black car dealer. While she thinks she is doing this on her own, this purchase, as well as a few other moments from the series, show how much contact Dr. Chegley has with Black Los Angeles. Chegley helped the dealer when his child was sick, so he owes Chegley a debt of gratitude, which he repays by reducing the price of the car that Julia purchases ("The Wheel Deal," s2:e2). Chegley also has a created an "inner city children's clinic," at which Julia volunteers one night a week. During the first season, one episode focuses on Chegley's attempts to raise money to keep the clinic open, which involves Julia going out to dinner with a potential donor—who happens to be a Black man who has some romantic interest in Julia. Even though Julia is not interested in him (thankfully she had the option to turn him down even if she was pushed to go out to dinner with him), he still gives more to the clinic than he was asked to give (s1:e25, "Takes Two to Tango").

Season 1's Christmas episode, "I'm Dreaming of a Black Christmas," is another episode that we can use to explore Julia's relationship with a larger Black community. There are moments that espouse a "color-blind" form of racism, such as when Chegley (who is visiting Julia at her apartment) says "when it comes to holidays, you folks sure go all out." The debate over whether Santa Claus is white or Black (between Corey and Earl) is mostly played for laughs, especially for an audience that knows that any Santa Claus is someone dressed up. That this episode touches at all on the idea that Black people might choose to represent Santa Claus as Black is a little surprising, and could be a touch of Carroll's own experience influencing the script. We see in this episode—which is later in the year—that Julia does have a few Black friends, one of whom agrees to dress up as Santa for Corey. While showing a Black character's connection to a Black world is not new (Beulah had an active life in the Black community), it is significant in the "multicultural" Los Angeles in which *Julia* takes place because the immediate, quotidian world in which Julia functions is not especially Black. While she does hire a young Black woman as Corey's babysitter, there isn't a sense of everyday presence of Black people in Corey's and Julia's lives. The conflict over whether or not Santa is Black prompts Julia to declare "It's times like this I wish everyone was beige. Or plaid. Especially Santa Claus."

Like so many other episodes, Kanter's world is structured through a lens of whiteness as the normative, and Black life and culture remain somewhat "alien." The appeal to a universal "plaid" coloring for everyone not only belies the reality of racial difference but emphasizes that everyone is the "same" even while acknowledging cultural differences between Black and white people. Chegley's voice is like that of Kanter, who sees the difference but never inquires about Black culture—why "you folks sure go all out" for the holiday. It sits, like so many other moments in the series, as an attempt to be "integrated" in a way that ultimately fails at being a culturally aware episode, even while it gives a glimpse into Black difference.

One example of Julia's engagement comes in the episode "You Can't Beat Drums" (S2:E7). In this instance, she engages more directly with another Black woman who has applied, and is approved, to live in her apartment building. The residents vote to approve the new potential tenants, Lydia Douglas and her family, which includes a teenage son, Lyle, and an absent father. The apartment is a culture in and of itself, and of course it has all sorts of unwritten rules, which Lydia breaks. First, she violates the unwritten code of the shared laundry room, then parks in the wrong parking space. And while the white residents of the building didn't have a problem with her, the fact that her son is a drummer, and practices with his band for hours in the afternoons, causes considerable friction.

The few people the drums don't seem to bother are Earl and Corey, who think the drums are cool, and Julia, because, of course, she is at work in the afternoon when Lyle is practicing. And none of the white residents wants to bring up the problem with Lydia, because they're afraid of being perceived as being prejudiced. Mr. Colton decides that they should have a meeting of all the residents at which they would politely confront Lydia about the noise. However, Lydia has come prepared, and has concluded that the other residents are ganging up on her, and that Julia is rude and unkind to her. She comes close to calling Julia a "sell-out." Clearly, the tensions in the building only increase with the meeting. Marking Julia as a "sell-out" brings an interesting moment of intraracial conflict to the show. On the one hand, both Julia and Lydia come across as firmly middle-class, making the characterization of "sell-out" seem odd. On the other hand, Julia's facility with the very white world of the building allies her with whiteness, at least to Lydia. The concept of a "sell-out" emerges in Black culture in the 1960s, so it is quite timely, and ironically the accusations of Julia being a sell-out will come to mirror how Black audiences and even Diahann Carroll herself see the show (Acham 2004).

This episode sets up the challenges of living day-to-day with the fear (on the part of the white building residents) of being assumed to be "prejudiced." All of the white apartment denizens are afraid to ask Lydia and Lyle to keep the noise down in large part because they fear a charge of prejudice. Lydia reacts to the well-meaning neighbors as someone whose experiences with racism make her suspicious of everyone. Of course, the white apartment residents do not object to Lydia and Lyle's presence. And once again, the writers slip in a reference to the times (however inaccurate it may be, historically). Of the smart and talented Lyle, who "could run for office," Mr. Colton says, "Until lately, a boy like Lyle couldn't even be a senator."[7] There is, of course, a solution to the problem of the drums; there is an unused room in the basement of the building that is essentially noise-proof, and an ideal setup for the band's practice. And the tension between Lydia and Julia disperses once the community solution is found.

Black Single Motherhood

While many sitcoms focus on either domestic or work situations, *Julia* spends time in both locations, work and home. We get some episodes that take up the challenges of being a single mother and a working mother, which we will address in this section. But before we take up some of the issues specific to Julia's home and work lives, we need to consider the fact of her Black single motherhood, and some of the implications of this particular representation on television in the late 1960s.[8]

The influence of the Moynihan Report (1965) was significant both in its policy implications and in terms of representation for Black women. The report, which was titled *The Negro Family: The Case for National Action*, was a product of Daniel Patrick Moynihan's work for the Department of Labor. Central to Moynihan's argument was that Black female-headed households were the key factor in the lack of "progress" of Black people in the United States. Moynihan articulated the notion of a Black "matriarch" as central in "dysfunctional" Black familial structures that contributed to the higher percentage of Black families that lived in poverty and relied on various types of public assistance. In other words, the persistence of Black poverty was an effect of Black women's "matriarchy" that, by implication, emasculated Black men and kept them from forming "proper" patriarchal family structures. The structural reasons for generational Black poverty were overshadowed, and this idea of "personal responsibility" emerged as a way to curtail certain kinds of programs to lift people out of poverty. Black feminists' engagement with the report points out that it ignored structural factors contributing to Blacks' lack of progress, and the detrimental effects that this report, and its characterizations of both Black men and Black women, have had on policy and practice.

Kanter's decision to make Julia a *widow* nominally takes her out of this discourse, because her single parenting is not by her choice. However, the fact that Kanter makes Julia a single mother I find problematic, especially in light of the discourse around Black families and single motherhood. While other Black fathers do make occasional appearances in the program, from the car dealer to a father at the free clinic, Kanter relinquishes the possibility of representing a Black nuclear middle-class family. If Julia had eventually remarried and provided Corey with a stepfather, Kanter might have had the opportunity to create a different kind of program. Julia does begin to date in the third season. Viewers are introduced to Steve Bruce in s3:e7, "Magna Cum Lover." This episode comes a few episodes after a moving episode in which Corey writes an essay to win a color TV. Corey chooses as his topic his father, who died when Corey was too young to remember him. The episode features pictures of Corey's father in uniform rather prominently, and his recounting of the essay (he wins third place—as the televisions were the prize for honorable mentions, he has done too well to get his television) brings tears to the eyes of his babysitter and Marie Waggedorn. Kanter and the writers walk a fine line here between a reverence for the lost soldier while engaging Julia with a serious love relationship. Played by former football star Fred Williamson in his first television role, Steve Bruce brings a somewhat regular Black male presence into the program. However, Steve and Julia don't marry; they consider eloping just before the end of the third and final season, so there isn't an opportunity for Steve to play a serious father figure role to Corey.

Julia is not the only character to appear as a single Black mother in the show. Lydia Douglas also appears as a single Black mother. While we eventually understand that Lydia's husband is on the road a lot as a musician, he isn't in the episode that features Lydia and her family. And in part because Julia's world is not focused or centered in a Black world, the television audience is left without a representation of a Black (nuclear) family in the show. While we do see extended family for Julia (a few cousins and relatives make appearances over the course of the series), we don't ever get a representation of a Black family more typical of the period.

Class

Class plays an interesting role in the series, in part because Kanter has deliberately chosen to place Julia in the "middle" class, in spite of her single parenthood. While usually Black middle-class people would be more likely to live in Black neighborhoods, Julia lives in a (nominally) integrated neighborhood in Los Angeles. As Isabel Wilkerson notes, in Chicago those who managed to move into the emergent Black middle class were still subject to "the color line [which] restricted them to the oldest housing in the least desirable section of town no matter what their class" (Wilkerson 2010). In Los Angeles, after the Great Migration (particularly in the postwar 1940s) saw Compton shift from being an almost exclusively white community to a majority city of color, Proposition 14 in 1965 overturned a previous fair housing act that penalized realtors who discriminated against Black homebuyers and renters. In the greater Los Angeles area, many cities were affected by restrictive covenants, including Venice and Huntington Park (Simpson 2012).

So we might say that *Julia* offers an optimistic look at integrated communities in Los Angeles in the late 1960s. And perhaps, Kanter is attempting to model a type of integration that might not have been present at the time, but might have existed in the near future. That Kanter sought to represent a Black middle class was laudable, even if his experience of it

Figure 2 Julia with Black friends.

was quite limited. Watching the show, however, we get a sense of Julia's hold on a middle-class status as somewhat precarious, and while her sensibilities are certainly middle class, her lifestyle is perhaps a lower middle-class status. Julia rents an apartment in a white/integrated neighborhood, but the apartment sometimes feels small for her and Corey. She owns a car; when her first car proves unreliable, she is able to purchase another used car with a bit of help. She cannot afford a color TV, as much as Corey might want one (in the third season). Vacations are occasional, and sometimes notable; she and Marie Waggedorn, along with Corey and Earl, venture to Las Vegas for her work colleague Hilda's wedding, but they cannot afford to stay long after the wedding.

As discussed briefly above, Julia has contact with a poor and working-class Black community in the "inner city" when she is working at the clinic that Chegley runs. But these moments feel exceptional in two ways; first, they are only occasionally points that drive plot for episodes, and second, they mark Julia and her education and class status as exceptional. We also see this kind of exceptionalism in the episode with the Bennetts. The episode marks a delineation between "those" Blacks, who live in ghettos and tenements, and Julia's kind (i.e., middle class) of Black people. Mr. Cooper, in his "argument" with Mrs. Bennett about her racism, cites several Black people who are "better" than he is (prejudice means you think you're better than other people), including Dr. Martin Luther King Jr., Ralph Bunche, and Hank Aaron. Thus even the liberal, open-minded Mr. Cooper recognizes the Black *exceptions.* So some Black people are okay, even if some of them live in tenements in the ghetto. While the push for integration is commendable (especially at a time when redlining was still prevalent and housing discrimination a reality), the script reveals the limits of the white writers in understanding the realities of Black lives, even middle-class Black lives, in the late 1960s (Figure 2). It's certainly possible that Julia would be allowed to integrate the building; her middle-class sensibilities and her facility in moving through a white world make her the "right kind" of tenant. Larger meanings still eluded our writers. In the world that they create for Julia, she has little contact with other Black people, and there is nothing in her apartment that looks culturally Black. Like her role in *No Strings*, Carroll is negotiating a white-imagined world in which she is "just like" the white people who are her neighbors and colleagues at work.

Hal Kanter's Racial Imaginary and
the Limits of Actor Influence

Hal Kanter imagined himself making up for the racist caricatures he participated in creating through his work on *The Beulah Show* and *Amos 'N' Andy* by presenting a sitcom with a middle-class Black woman as the protagonist. Hiring Diahann Carroll to play Julia created (to a point) the possibility of input and developing a character that would accurately reflect Black middle-class life in the United States. To the degree to which he was able to hear Carroll's discussion of Black middle-class life, the show did get some things right.

As much as *Julia* renounced the same tired stereotypes that were endemic during this time, it made fewer advances than it might. By the time the third season concluded, Carroll had grown frustrated with Kanter and her inability to make the kinds of substantive changes in the show that would have more accurately reflected Black middle-class life. Black audiences, who seemed eager for programming that presented nonstereotyped characters, quickly tired of *Julia*, and by its end were writing asking for its cancellation. In the late 1960s, in the middle of the most activist time of the Civil Rights movement, *Julia* became acutely out of touch with current events. Kanter's insistence on "prejudice" as an individual failing did not accurately reflect the realities for Black people. To make Julia's close friend Leonard Waggedorn an LAPD officer runs contrary to the deep racism of the LAPD during the period. The civil unrest that emerged out of the Vietnam War protests and the Civil Rights movement seem to not touch Julia's life, except for the fact of her husband's death in Vietnam.

That *Julia* explicitly excludes (yet again) a Black father figure for young Corey reflects a white imaginary that always sees Black families as incomplete, and that cannot find a way to imagine Black masculinity as an enduring presence in the lives of Julia and Corey. While single parenting because of the death of a spouse was not uncommon (*Family Affair*, for example) during the period, Kanter's inability to create a father figure for Corey reveals the contours, and the limits, of a white-imagined Black family. For all of her cachet earned through her Tony award and her popularity with audiences, Carroll was limited in her ability to fully recreate a Black middle-class *family* on television. Black audiences emerged with sharp critiques of the program, and combined with Carroll's growing frustration with Kanter, the show was concluded after the third season. The critiques laid heavily on Carroll's consciousness, and she grew tired and frustrated at having to work to keep material that was either unaware or even tacitly racist out of the scripts. As with the example about Julia's first experience with racism, Kanter grew reluctant to make changes to his idea of Julia. Carroll's frustration mounted, and the stress began to take its toll. Ultimately, "when, in 1970, the time came to renew my contract again, I decided to ask for my release. I was exhausted. I had had, to put it simply, enough" (Carroll and Firestone 1986, 163). With no Carroll, there would be no *Julia*.

Representing the Black middle class made it easy to avoid some of the pitfalls that came, and will come again, with representing the Black working class. So many of the things endemic to the stereotype fall away; dialect, crime, victimhood, and lack of education and opportunities are neatly avoided, for the most part, in Kanter's made-up Los Angeles. White audiences get to see a part of Black life that they didn't necessarily know existed. But instead of surrounding Julia with a Black community that had a mixture of socioeconomic classes, we get an "integrated" Los Angeles where it seems Julia's community is primarily her white neighbors and colleagues. She has limited contact in the show with the Black working class (only in the free clinic that Chegley runs, at which she volunteers a few nights a week). She also has limited contact with a coherent Black middle class. While she knows of Black car salesmen and other businesspeople, she is not depicted as having sustained, engaged relationships with other Black middle-class people. She doesn't seem to belong to a civic organization like a sorority or Black women's club, things that were hallmarks of Black middle-class life in the late 1960s, and Corey's world seems completely white. For Black audiences, at a time when there is so much activism and resistance, *Julia* feels integrationist, assimilationist—the epitome of the "sell-out." Carroll's frustration with Kanter's increasing resistance to her efforts to get the representation "right" would seal *Julia*'s fate. Fortunately, we would not have to wait another decade before new situation comedies about Black life would premiere, but this kind of representation of the Black middle class would disappear for more than a decade.

For her part, Carroll would not be done with television. Her most significant and enduring role would be that of Dominique Devereaux on *Dynasty* from 1984 to 1989. She would later appear on several of the other programs we will discuss later, including *A Different World* (nine episodes, where she played Whitley's mother) and *Grey's Anatomy*. Her television persona was cemented with both the *Julia* and *Dynasty* roles, and she would go on to play many glamorous Black "lady" characters throughout the rest of her career, until her death in 2019.

Not Such "Good Times": The Limits of Black Actors' Influence

In the previous chapters I have argued that Black women actors, whose acting careers prior to moving to television were sufficiently recognized through various awards, influenced (to a point) representations of their own and other Black characters on the television programs in which they starred. From the beginnings of television until the 1970s, these opportunities were few and far between. As a result, both *The Beulah Show* and *Julia* served as exemplars of the possibilities, within the television context, of creating or shifting representations that departed from the common stereotypes of Hollywood, whether television or film. As the only programs with Black women in leading roles, *Beulah* and *Julia* offered something different, while they lasted. In both cases, the changes were limited, and in both cases, a time came when the programs lost their novelty and/or support from the networks and Black audiences alike.

While *Beulah's* production was mired in the racial politics (and stereotypes) of the 1950s, and *Julia's* production was limited by Kanter's unwillingness to more deeply understand the world of middle-class African Americans, both tried to offer a glimpse into Black life for television audiences. Both show featured prominent Black women stage actors, giving audiences hope that they would move beyond stereotypes; in this, both had some minor successes, but ultimately failed. In the 1970s, some of the most iconic situation comedies would be produced, and as a result, additional opportunities emerged for Black-centered programming. Would the third time be the charm?

The "Golden Age" of Situation Comedy

We might mark the 1970s as a golden age of television situation comedy. This is the era of the Norman Lear comedy and the era in which situation comedy took up significant social issues, including abortion (*Maude*), racism, interracial marriage (*The Jeffersons*), class issues, sexism, feminism, and progressive politics. Lear's politics were left-leaning, as is quite evident from the social issues that his sitcoms addressed. *All in the Family* initiated a sitcom dynasty, as it spawned not only *Maude* but *The Jeffersons* and, tangentially, *Good Times*. Initially Florida Evans was a character on *Maude* who was Maude's maid. This character was changed slightly, moved to Chicago, and became the matriarch of the Evans family in *Good Times*. Within the programs that Lear produced, there were two programs that focused on Black life: *The Jeffersons*, on the Bunkers's former neighbors who "move up" to an upper middle-class position and high-rise apartment in Manhattan, and *Good Times*, on a working-class Black family in Chicago.

Good Times ran for six seasons. For its first four seasons, it ranked in the Nielsen top programs; in its first season, it was seventeenth; in its second season, it ranked seventh; in its third season, twenty-fourth; and in its fourth season, twenty-sixth. After its fourth season, it dropped out of the top of the ratings. We will return to the issue of ratings later; we can see certain contours of the show shift, and the changes in ratings may be both indicative and a result of those changes. The era of *Good Times* included other Black-themed programming, including *Sanford and Son*, *The Jeffersons*, *What's Happening*, and *Diff'rent Strokes*. Among these programs, all of which were in the top of the Nielsen ratings, *Good Times* stands alone as a sitcom about a working-class nuclear family.[1] With *The Jeffersons* we have a nuclear family, more or less, since their son is an adult, but they are not working class. *Sanford and Son* similarly is essentially about a father and son; *What's Happening* features a single mother, and *Diff'rent Strokes* features the adoption of two Black brothers by a wealthy white man. We will focus here on *Good Times* for two reasons. First, like McDaniel and Carroll, Esther Rolle (who played Florida Evans) had a significant stage career before turning to television. Second, Rolle's work on *Good Times* duplicates some of the struggles and challenges of the actors in the previous decades. She was central to *Good Times* and worked to make some changes in the program. As we shall see, she also grew frustrated with her inability to change the program for the better.

The United States during the mid-1970s was a contested space. While it did not have the overt volatility of the mid- to late 1960s, it had its share of social and political shifts within the culture. This is also true for Black life during the period, one that saw some significant growth in a Black middle class but also white flight from urban to suburban contexts, complex negotiations culturally around the effects of the Civil Rights movement, and the retrenchment of poverty in the inner cities. The 1970s saw extended interracial conflict over school segregation in Boston; between 1974 and 1976, there were protests and riots. While the conflict in Boston was the most extreme example, busing conflicts emerged in various cities across the country. School integration was one of the issues that contributed to "white flight," in which white residents of cities either moved to nearby suburbs or placed their children in private rather than public schools.

School integration was not the only integration issue in the early to mid-1970s. The same suburbs that had been exclusively white, sometimes with covenants and restrictions, saw an influx of Black families who could, because of a rising Black middle class, afford to purchase homes in these neighborhoods. The rise of a visible Black middle class can also be attributed to the changes wrought by the Civil Rights movement, especially the Civil Rights Act of 1964 and the ways in which new employment opportunities opened up. In particular, civil service positions with city, state, and federal government expanded job opportunities for Blacks, and these positions, with their regular salaries and benefits, enabled some to economically move into the middle class (Newman 2000).

The increased Black presence on television in the 1970s follows a general increase in Black visibility in various places within US culture. School, workplace, and neighborhood desegregation meant that there was a tangible increased Black presence in the lives of many whites. These demographic shifts may partially account for the popularity of Black-themed programming on the major networks, whether in sitcoms focused on Black characters or the integration of Black characters into other types of programming, such as police procedurals and other workplace-focused programs.

For Black working-class people, the 1970s saw increasing unemployment, and Blacks bore a heavier burden of the economic struggles during the period, which included high inflation and the oil crisis. While all Americans were affected by higher rates of unemployment, Blacks historically and indeed in this period were more significantly impacted (a high of 14.8 percent unemployment in 1975, according to the Bureau of Labor Statistics). In inner cities in particular, where unemployment rates were higher, this meant that the socioeconomic status of most Blacks did not improve during the 1970s. The lingering effects of the Moynihan Report continued to place the "blame" for inner city poverty on Black single mothers. In 1974, articles in *Jet* magazine and the *Chicago Tribune* coined the term "welfare queen" to describe welfare fraud, using the single case of a woman named Linda Taylor, who collected welfare under several different names. The idea of the "welfare queen" who collected multiple checks and got "rich" off welfare may have been a rare if not single occurrence, but once it was used by Ronald Reagan in his 1976 presidential campaign, the myth created a new controlling image of Black women. Following so closely on the heels of Moynihan's Black matriarch, the two images—of the Black matriarch and the welfare queen—combined to solidify a social and political concept of the Black single mother becoming rich by living off of welfare, emasculating Black men, and simultaneously bearing responsibility for a "culture of poverty." The term "culture of poverty" (or subculture of poverty) was first used by Oscar Lewis in an essay about intergenerational poverty that was published in Daniel Patrick Moynihan's edited volume *On Understanding Poverty: Perspectives from the Social Sciences* (NY: Basic Books, 1969). The notion that poverty is an individual failing has been refuted by scholars who understand poverty as structural. The fact that this essay appeared in an anthology edited by Moynihan, in the years following Lyndon Johnson's "war on poverty," solidify the *meaning* of single Black motherhood among poor urban people of color as one of the undeserving poor, who are lazy and only interested in taking what they can from the government.

When Rolle began working on *Maude*, she was very aware of this particular image of Black women that had recently emerged in the popular consciousness. Because of her political and social awareness, she was determined to not contribute to the perpetuation of this particular myth of Black womanhood. As we will see in the next section, her theatrical training contributed to her having a political consciousness about her work as an actor. That consciousness would shape her work on *Good Times* and, like other Black actors with similar perspectives, would influence her role choice and work for her career.

Esther Rolle's Theatrical Background

Rolle's theatrical background is significant, as it bears on her ability to be cast as Florida, initially in the *Maude* series and then not only for the creation of *Good Times* as a vehicle for Florida Evans but also in some of the specific artistic decisions made at the beginning of the series. Like many of the other actors in this book, Rolle came to television with a successful career on the stage. She was trained as a dancer, and an early important stage role was in the 1962 Off-Broadway production of *The Blacks*. As an early member of the Negro Ensemble Company (NEC), Rolle regularly performed in New York. She had a strong reputation in the New York theatre world, so much so that she was called "that Mount Rushmore of a performer" by Walter Kerr (Richards 1986). The importance of her being a part of the NEC cannot be understated. The NEC was the preeminent Black theatre troupe in New York in the 1960s and the place where much of the burgeoning Black theatre of the time was produced. This was the theatre that produced (and Esther Rolle performed in) Douglas Turner Ward's satires *Day of Absence* (about a Southern town that wakes to find all of its Black people have disappeared) and *Happy Endings* (which flips the stereotype of the Black maid/housekeeper who cares more for the white family than her own on its head). She was cast in Derek Wolcott's *Dream on Monkey Mountain* and in two James Baldwin plays, *Blues for Mister Charlie* and *The Amen Corner*, both of which would bring her to Broadway. Being a regular within this particular Black theatre world means that Rolle had considerable training with some of the most well-known and skilled actors of the time and that she "grew up" in theatre focused on Black artistic production and a pan-African Black history and literature. Rolle's social and political sense developed and refined as a result of her work at the NEC.

The NEC's work was, in the words of Ellen Foreman, "transcendent" (Foreman 1980). Founded in part by Douglas Turner Ward, the NEC "reflected the Black nationalism of the sixties but also transcended it" (271). With collaborators Robert Hooks and Gerald Krone, Ward secured a Ford Foundation grant for $1,200,000 to create a company that included a training program to develop Black talent and allow them to produce their first three seasons of shows. Along with Ed Cambridge, Rosalind Cash, and Moses Gunn, Esther Rolle was one of the first group of theatre artists who began the NEC. The NEC was not the most radical of Black theatre troupes in the late 1960s and early 1970s, but it was one of the most critically acclaimed. As Foreman asserts, NEC

> "forg[ed] its own multifaceted identity, [...] with its first three years present[ing] drama of pan-African sweep: American, Caribbean and African perspectives, of astonishing range and quality, in a dazzling array of outlooks, moods, and styles, offering the broadest possible definition of Black experience."
>
> (275)

The climate of the NEC meant that Rolle had broad experience with a range of Black dramatic traditions that were Black-created performance. Just prior to entering television, she was the lead in Melvin Van Peebles's play, *Don't Sell Us Cheap.*[2]

She landed her first television role as a maid named Florida Evans in Lear's *Maude*. On *Maude*, she would continue to be surrounded by stage actors of highly developed skill, particularly Bea Arthur, who was a veteran Broadway performer before she took on *Maude*. Rolle was well aware of the "mammy" stereotype that haunted the representational arts and was determined that she would not play the role of Florida Evans as a stereotype: "eventually, Lear convinced her that the role on Maude would be different from that of the stereotypical Hollywood representation of the domestic. In her acceptance of the character, Rolle acknowledged what she thought her position in television could do" (Acham 2004, 128). Acham quotes Rolle from a *TV Guide* interview:

> I've always been very unhappy about the role of domestics. The black woman in America doesn't need to go to drama school to be a maid. The old actresses who played the black maid stereotypes are not villains—it's the ones who hired them. We have been stereotyped and unrecognized for too long. Anyone who digs in the earth or scrubs somebody's floor—I don't blame them for taking that job, I ache that they had to do it.
>
> (John Riley, "Esther Rolle the Fishin' Pole," TV Guide, 29 June 1974, quoted in Acham 2004, 128)

As Acham notes, Rolle was very aware of the impacts of representation on both Black and white viewers. Particularly for white viewers, a limited number of representations of Black people, particularly Black women, allows the mythologies of Blackness to be perpetuated; while integration more broadly in US society in the 1970s meant that more whites came into contact with Blacks on a daily basis in a variety of roles, it was all too easy to slip into the facile, undifferentiated notions of Blackness that reinforce myths like those of the Black matriarch and the welfare queen. At this particular time, it was important for Rolle to strive to create something different in her work in television, to push against those notions of Blackness:

> Rolle's actions also represent a cognizance of the impact of the Moynihan Report, which branded the black family as dysfunctional. Rolle refused to participate in furthering this legacy by placing the image of the matriarchal black family into the media forum and instead presented what she believed to be an uplifting image of the black family.
>
> (Acham 2004, 129)

Richards describes Rolle's role on *Maude* as "the back-talking maid, who chastened Bea Arthur's liberalism with a dash of common sense" (1986, B1). Her popularity on *Maude* led to Lear creating another vehicle for her, one in which she would be starring; she certainly had star appeal. Once she got Norman Lear to agree to have a father in the family, she was satisfied with it. In an interview, she said, "in the beginning, I loved the series. It was a thing of worth—the first time you saw a black family on TV, husband included. Everything else up to that time was a mother and her children, as if the black husband just didn't exist" (Richards 1986). Lear had initially thought of Florida Evans as a single mother; while Lear's progressive credentials might have led him to think differently about how he would construct Florida's family, it had not occurred to him when pitching *Good Times* to Rolle that by making this a single-parent family, he was buying into stereotypes about urban Black America. It was only because of Rolle's pressure to include a father that one was included, even if only for the first few years. Without a father present, the program would reflect the negative stereotypes associated with Black families (and historically, the lack of representation of Black families in situation comedy, as was the case in *Julia*, would continue).

While clearly Rolle is important for her portrayal of Florida, I am also interested in the representation of a Black *family*, since until this point, there has not been a representation of a Black nuclear family in this context.[3] I am also interested in how this first Black *family* sitcom deals with Black masculinities, especially because the actors John Amos and Jimmie Walker, and the roles they played, became so controversial. Let us consider, then, the first season of *Good Times*.

Good-ish Times—First Season

We get a clear sense of what *Good Times* will be from the very first episode of the series. The Evans family is a family of five: James Sr., played by John Amos, is the father; Florida, his wife (at the beginning of the series she does not work outside the home); James Jr., otherwise known as J. J., the eldest son, who is in high school and an artist; Thelma, the only daughter, also in high school and who wants to become a doctor; and Michael, the youngest, still in elementary school, and who wants to become a Supreme Court justice. The five live in a two-bedroom, one-bathroom apartment in Chicago, likely the Cabrini-Green housing projects.

The key plot in the first episode is that James has received a letter letting him know that he is eligible for a training program that will land him a union job making $4.25 an hour, a veritable fortune in 1970s dollars. This job will set the Evans family up; it holds the potential for them to access the "American Dream," to move out of their housing project and no longer struggle to make ends meet.

The possibility of moving to a home where two of their children did not have to sleep on the couch would have been a boon. In anticipation of James's new job, Florida plans a party, complete with champagne. We already know, though, that this job is not going to pan out for James. So it is not really a surprise when we discover that James has to miss out on this opportunity because of a clerical error—he is too old for the program. After he reveals to the assembled group that he didn't get the job, James and Florida have a private conversation:

> Florida: It's ain't all that bad, James. This family has stood up to a whole lot of dream smashing.
> James: Yeah. I thought if I'da got that job, we was going to be okay. Instead, we broke.
> Florida: What was we yesterday?
> James: Broke.
> Florida: And probably will be again tomorrow. But James, you always see this family through. You can do it.
> James: That's my baby. So I missed out. What's the big deal? What would it have meant anyhow? Some more spending money, fancy clothes, a nicer place to live? What I need a union job for when I got you and these kids? Huh?
> Florida: You don't.
> James: You better believe that. But it sure would have been nice.

James does get some work; his neighbor gets him a job at Al's Car Wash, and he works a second job in order to provide for the family. Where one door closes, another opens. Florida's role here is as supportive of James and his struggles; even in this episode, we see a sharp contrast to the notion of the Black matriarch, who was constructed as hostile to Black men and detrimental to Black masculinity. Florida is hardly the emasculating matriarch; this is established clearly in this first episode. Rolle's portrayal of Florida creates a tone for the series. While not necessarily playing into "respectability politics," Rolle's screen presence creates a humanized Black family that exists in contrast to the other programming on television, and in contrast to the images of poor and working-class Blacks in inner cities.

Aesthetically, there are some important features of the characters and how they are presented, especially in this first episode (and through the first two seasons) that will change as the years go by. Both Florida and Thelma wear their hair natural; Florida's short afro gives her a look of dignified middle-age, while Thelma's cornrows speak to a Black aesthetic of the time. Only Willona does not wear her hair natural, and in the early years it appears she is wearing a wig rather than having her hair straightened (Figure 3). This is one of those moments where the influence of those steeped in Black culture—Rolle, as well as Amos and Eric Monte, who grew up in Cabrini-Green and is one of the show's creators, makes its presence felt through a modicum of verisimilitude, even in a situation comedy. We would see some of this consciousness fall away over the course of the series; while Rolle only ever wears her hair in a short afro, Thelma and Willona will go through several different types of hairstyles.

Our introduction to the Evans family thus captures how the showrunners imagine Black family life. As Coleman points out, in *Good Times*, the Evans family largely operates in a Black world—it is not an unrealistic segregation, but is a segregation nonetheless. She notes, "Blacks operated in separate, unequal worlds from Whites [...] [Lear's] comedies, at minimum, reflected a devastating societal trend, and in the fullest degree reinforced an unequal separation and segregation in which it was communicated that Whites and Blacks cannot, should not, and will not coexist" (1998, 88).

The topics that *Good Times* engaged during the first three seasons reflected important aspects of African American life in the mid-1970s. Throughout the first season and the first half of the second season, Florida does not work; in keeping with trends in the mid-1970s, however, the family gains slightly more

Figure 3 Esther Rolle and BernNadette Stanis with natural hair.

financial stability when there is more than one income (especially as James is vulnerable to layoffs in this climate of high unemployment). Among the topics covered in the first two seasons are gang activity, encounters with the police and the justice system, school busing and standardized testing, unemployment, women's rights, poverty, and hunger. In one episode, J. J. is the victim of mistaken identity and arrested for armed robbery, with its concomitant issues of money bail and mass incarceration (the episode still resonates today, when these issues have become even more prominent); Michael is chosen to be bused to a more affluent school in a white neighborhood; the Evans's neighbor faces hunger. Other plots concerned adoption, drug addiction, family estrangement, and political differences within families. As Amos said in an interview, Norman Lear gave people "something I can relate to, family problems" (Amos 2014).

No matter what things are thrown their way, James and Florida will manage to keep the family afloat in these circumstances. While the genre dictates that issues are resolved in an episode (sometimes two), and most of the endings are ostensibly "happy" ones, we never forget the precarity of the Evans's lives, and the challenges of being working class and Black in America. Using several episodes as exemplars, the next sections will consider some of the themes that emerged on the first three seasons of the show. The show ran for six years, and all episodes are available. From a list of episode story lines, I chose episodes from each season that stood out because of their plots or because they were particularly good examples of the themes that would be explored in multiple episodes over the course of the show's run.

Black History and Culture

Young Michael is the revolutionary of the family; in that, he is the voice of Black resistance in the 1970s. We can expect, therefore, that Michael is often the butt of the jokes that deal explicitly with racism. His father refers to him as the "militant midget," and even when he tries to agitate for improving their circumstances and against institutional racism, his parents often admonish him for his efforts. In season 1, episode 5, he comes home early in the day when he clearly should be at school. He explains that he has been suspended because he insisted to his teacher that "George Washington was a white racist."

Florida: What?!
Michael: Well, he was, Mama, he owned slaves!

Florida: You little squirt! Where do you come off calling the father of our country a racist? Where'd you pick up such trash?

Michael: In the library. In a book on Black History.

Florida: Well you still don't say things like that about George Washington. If you had to insult somebody you should have played it safe and picked on someone like Benedict Arnold.

Michael: Mama, I'm just telling it like it is.

Florida: Boy—

Michael: Mama, "boy" is a white racist word.

Florida: This boy is so black I'm going to have to lead a protest march before he'll say I'm his mama!

Both Florida and James respond largely negatively to Michael's suspension, both because of his intelligence and because his "revolutionary" attitude could potentially get him into trouble. James and Florida insist that Michael apologize to the teacher; failing that, James intends to spank Michael. But Michael's educational discussion with James keeps him from getting a spanking and enlightens his father, and the audience, on some key points in Black history. In a later episode, Michael writes a letter to the *Chicago Defender* about the state of disrepair of their housing project. On the one hand, at least these sentiments are present; on the other hand, they are marked as "radical" and are cause for laughter for the audience. This early episode also highlights one of Rolle's persistent problems with the character of J. J. While he is an accomplished artist, he also disdains learning. He could have been a role model as an artist, but his pride in his lack of education contributes to him as a negative stereotype.

The references and calls to a rich African American culture do come up in the program, at least during the first two seasons. Michael's voice is that of a kind of "Black power," even if it is sometimes the punch line of a joke. The reference to the *Chicago Defender*, one of the oldest and most-read Black newspapers in the country (it was founded in 1905), is a clear reference to Black Chicago and its history. At a time when many Black women were straightening their hair, both Esther Rolle's Florida Evans and BernNadette Stanis's Thelma wear their hair natural, which is as radical in a way as Michael's Black consciousness-raising efforts (Byrd and Tharps 2014; Patton 2006; Weitz 2001). During the 1970s, as Black women moved into work in more public spaces (as opposed to private/domestic spaces), there was pressure to straighten or relax their hair. For a television example, Isabel Sanford on *The Jeffersons* wears her hair in a short relaxed or straightened style. Thelma's longer hair gets creative natural styles. In another episode, Florida responds to Thelma's fantasizing about Billy Dee Williams by recalling similar movie-star fantasies—for white actors. "In those days, those were the only men we could dream about. It was either Errol Flynn and Clark Gable, or Stepin Fetchit and Rochester! Somehow the sword seemed more dashing than the broom" (s1:e5). For all that J. J. is (even from the beginning of the series) a classic "coon" type of character, the paintings that are "his" work in the series are actually by the African American artist Ernie Barnes, who captured Black sensibilities in his work.[4] Series cocreator, Eric Monte, was himself a product of the Cabrini-Green housing projects and was strongly opposed in general to negative depictions of Blacks on television (Taylor 2014). While listed as a cocreator for the entire series, Monte's only writing credits for the show are episodes during the first season.

Black Feminist Content

At the beginning of season 2, the first episode treats us to a strongly feminist episode. Florida has been in a bad mood for several days, and the episode opens with Michael asking about menopause, thinking his mother has "caught" it. Florida's malaise becomes obvious moments later, when she enters the scene and proceeds to yell at all three of her children before taking the laundry downstairs to the building laundry room. Just beneath the surface, though, we see what Florida's problem might be; Thelma is supposed to be helping with making breakfast but leaves the oatmeal on the stove, and it nearly burns; J. J. is still in his pajamas, and Michael has yet to make up the pull-out couch that is his and J. J.'s bed.

Florida meets Willona in the hallway on the way to the laundry room. Willona has an idea about what is bothering Florida and suggests that Florida come with her to her "women's meeting." As a divorced woman, Willona has been to the meetings many times, and the group's consciousness raising has helped her to get through her divorce. Florida resists going to the meeting, insisting there is nothing wrong with her. Willona makes her excuses and goes to talk to James about what's bothering Florida:

Willona: She doesn't have enough to do.
James: I let her do all the washing, cleaning, scrubbing, sewing,
    shopping—I ain't the kind of man that interferes with a woman's pleasure.
Willona: That's very white of you.

Willona's assertion here might seem odd, but was marked as a laugh line. Willona is implying that James's treatment of Florida is like the way that white men view white women; not fully regarding Florida as a partner but as someone who essentially works for him. This sentiment is starkly different from the Black feminism of the Combahee River Collective, whose 1974 statement is contemporaneous with the show. The scene continues:

> Willona: James, you go off to work, the kids go off to school, you don't see her the way I do. She spends her whole life trying to stretch two dreary hours of work into the big nothing of a day.
>
> James: What?
>
> Willona: You think cooking and sewing and washing is Florida's thing? She's wasting herself, James. It's an empty existence.

In the first season, Florida doesn't work but seems nominally content in her life as a housewife. The second season becomes, in part, the season in which Florida "finds herself" and begins to come into herself, especially as her children grow up and need her less for day-to-day care. Florida acquiesces and goes to Willona's women's meeting. The concerns expressed there are firmly rooted in Black feminist awareness; first, the leader of the group discusses how Black women's needs are different from white women's needs (wanting to free themselves from the typewriter) and the broader issues that Black women face, including physical and verbal abuse (unfortunately played for laughs). While not as radical as organizations like Combahee, this mild version of Black feminism still makes points about labor and physical abuse that were common during the period. Florida doesn't see herself as having much in common with these women; after all, as she asserts, her marriage is fine, and her husband certainly wouldn't think that women "belong in two places—the kitchen and the bedroom." She returns home, where the family has been worried about her, and for a short time things are good, until James asserts his masculinity and becomes angry about the women's meeting. When James responds in their argument with the same line that Florida heard in the women's meeting, she realizes that perhaps what plagues her is not so different what that other Black women are also trying to manage (the goal of consciousness-raising groups). Florida tells him, "I made you and the kids my life, and now I have no life of my own. I want to be somebody, too."

One of the things that I find interesting about the narrative of Black women (and Black feminism) that this episode asserts is that it is predicated on a family model that was not necessarily common among Black households (particularly in the South, where Black women could work as domestics when jobs for Black men were scarce, but also in urban environments). Florida's home life in the early years of the series is one that many Black women who were employed outside of the home in "pink collar" jobs—mostly likely as domestics, but also in other kinds of service roles—would have been happy for. Florida's discontent with being a housewife echoes the feminist narrative of white middle-class women, particularly as outlined by Betty Friedan's *The Feminine Mystique*. Particularly among Black working-class women, it was not out of the ordinary that they would work outside of the home. When Florida begins first to educate herself by taking classes and working to get her G. E. D., and then proceeds to land a job outside of the home, she is more in line with the experiences of many working-class Black women. Where this was less true is in places where Black men could access union factory or civil service jobs, that paid better and had better benefits. In those instances, working-class or lower-middle-class Blacks might well have had a single, rather than multiple, source of income within the family.

The Show Begins to Change

For three years, Amos and Rolle somewhat collaboratively worked with the showrunners and writers to infuse the show with various topics that reflected of Black culture. While they may or may not have lobbied together, they had similar feelings about the show's direction. It was also clear, from the second season on, that the character of J. J. became more prominent, and his signature "Dy-no-Mite!" became increasingly exaggerated and common. In the third season, while the majority of the episodes (eight of twenty-four) focus on Florida (four), James (one), or the two of them (three), there are six episodes that feature J. J., far more than Thelma (three) or Michael (two). The first season had more episodes focused on either James or J. J. than any of the other main characters. In the second season, a significant number of episodes focuses on J. J. (seven of twenty-four), with four each for Michael, Florida, and James (Thelma gets the short shrift, with only two episodes that focus on her). The episodes focused on J. J. in the first two seasons take on subjects like gang violence and encounters with law enforcement, while later episodes focus in a variety of ways on J. J.'s love life, even when the topics (heroin addiction, STIs) are the social issue of the episode.

With season 3, the show got new executive producers, Austin and Irma Kalish, and it was in part their influence that moved J. J. to the prime spot. They also felt that the episodes should continue to show important issues—"drugs and gangs and venereal disease and the current multipart story on child abuse as examples of meaningful subject matter" (Margulies 1977). But clearly while these are important issues, they are not the same kinds of issues that were featured in the first two seasons of the show. They also reflect a white imaginary of the inner city Black experience, and the dearth of episodes devoted to Black history or culture marks a break from the early episodes of the show. The following themes emerge in the show's third season.

Making James Expendable

As we look into the plots for episodes in season 3, a couple of things become noticeable. First, there is already a decrease in the number of episodes that include James; he is out of town several times. Episode 9, "The Politicians," constructs James in a somewhat conservative way during a clash between old and new. James and the rest of the family argue over the candidates in the local ward election. While James supports the incumbent, who has represented their ward for twenty years, Florida, Willona, and the children support the young candidate who envisions a different future for the population of the projects, one that sees Black progress in a city where that has largely not been possible.[5]

Lowered Expectations

In several instances, the expectations or aspirations of the youngest members of the cast are either falling away or otherwise changing. In episode 4, "Love in the Ghetto," James is once again in conflict with the family over Thelma's engagement to her 20-year-old boyfriend, Larry. As Florida works to convince James to approve of the engagement, she spends much of the episode recounting their courtship and the early years of their marriage. Florida can see Thelma's attraction to Larry; he is much like James. James, on the other hand, resists because he, like many parents, wants Thelma's life to be easier than his, which cannot happen if she marries young and does not go to college as they have planned. It is also in season 3 that Michael's aspirations are downgraded; in episode eight, "Michael's Big Fall," Michael hides his report card from the family because, for the first time in his life, he did not get all As. Having recently been enrolled in a new school and a kind of talented/gifted program, Michael no longer feels that he is smarter than everyone. When Florida goes to talk with his teacher, she is convinced that they should let Michael decide what he wants to do, even if that is not the path they wanted for him. What I find most interesting about this episode is that in the first season, it is Michael who says he wants to sit on the Supreme Court; in season 3, he makes a statement that it was his parents who wanted that for him. This makes for a stark contrast between what is established in the first season and what emerges with the new producers in season 3. Either there is a lack of continuity (or a lack of caring about continuity), or the show has shifted to be something different. This change in the "story" of the family is not true to Eric Monte's vision, if we take things that were established in that first season as part of his vision. Florida articulates in the first season her desire for her children to do better than she and James did. This change means that any aspirations for the Evanses can only ever be thwarted. As the ghetto is constructed in the white imaginary, and at this point also in the series, as generational, it is therefore not something people are generally given to "escape." What *Good Times* shows to audiences is that people don't really "escape" the ghetto, that even when given choices to get more education, Blacks will get distracted from those goals.

This is not to draw focus away from the important social issues the show continues to take up through the first three seasons nor to detract from the importance of Rolle in the show (both in terms of her representation of Florida and her influence on the show's aesthetics and politics). Rather, I see this as reflecting the way the show's writers and producers understood the popularity of the character of J. J., while diminishing the importance of the character of James in particular. While Florida remains a prominent feature of the program, there is a direct relationship between the increase in episodes focused on J. J. and the decrease in episodes focused on James. John Amos and Esther Rolle were both outspoken about their objections to the reliance on Jimmie Walker's (J. J.) brand of comedy (coming from stand-up), which was significantly different from the stage acting (drama and comedy) of Rolle and, to a lesser degree, Amos. Outspoken critiques of the show by Amos and Rolle led to tensions with the showrunners, leading to significant changes for the show's fourth season.

Goodbye James, Goodbye Florida, Goodbye Consciousness

During the hiatus between the third and fourth seasons, Norman Lear let John Amos know that he was being fired from the show. Amos says that it was in part because he was not very diplomatic when confronting the writers and producers about the direction the show was taking.

I felt with two other younger children, one of whom aspired to be a supreme court justice, […] and BernNadette Stanis, she aspired to be a surgeon. And the differences I had with the producers of the show, I felt too much emphasis was being put on J.J. and his chicken hat [a hat with a chicken on top], and saying 'Dy-no-mite' every third page, when just as much emphasis and mileage could have been gotten out of my other two children and the concomitant jokes and humor that could have come out of that.

(Amos 2014)

Amos's James first lands a better job in Mississippi (episode 1 of season 4), and in the second episode, the family gets word of his death. The shift to J. J. being the primary character on the show seems to happen quickly, and he clearly dominates the plots for the fourth season.

Esther Rolle would soon follow Amos off the show. While Rolle was more diplomatic than Amos, she too tired of the broad "coon" version of Blackness that Walker embodied: "Rolle in particular used the press to create vocal counternarratives to the presentations on the screen when they did not meet her personal standards. This is why, as a whole, *Good Times* is politically contested terrain in which contradictory meanings often occurred" (Acham 2004, 132–3). As the fourth season continued, Rolle was more and more emphatic that Walker's character be toned down. Of the twenty-four episodes in the fourth season, eleven (nearly half) of them focused on J. J. Three are focused on Michael; one a plot related to gangs, one in which he attempts to sing with a group in a talent show, and one in which a girl he likes falls for J. J. Thelma, who wanted to become a surgeon, is in college in season 4 but is suspended for taking part in a protest, then nearly leaves college to marry. The show's fourth season shifted decidedly away from the show that it was during the first three seasons. Rolle had worked hard to make the show into something that she could be proud of; once Amos had left, she worked harder to get her opinion about the show's new trajectory into the press. In an interview in *Ebony* in 1975, Rolle stated commented that "He (J. J.) is 18 and he doesn't work. He can't read or write. He doesn't think. The show didn't start out to be that. Michael's role of a bright, thinking child has been subtly reduced […] I resent the imagery that says to black kids that you can make it by standing on the corner saying 'Dy-no-mite!'" Rather than Amos's directly confrontational style, Rolle tried a softer approach; while she voiced her discontent to the writers, producers, and to Lear himself, she relied on statements made to the press to do the work of contesting the show's new producers and new focus. In spite of their conflict, however, the show wasn't interested in firing Rolle.

With so much of the show focused on J. J. and on plots that emphasized his get-rich-quick schemes, Rolle's disappointment led her to leave. Rolle said after leaving the show,

> I rather disliked, was unhappy about, the changes that were coming about in the show. If there is no quality, if there is no integrity, if there is nothing that I cannot feel ashamed of your child watching, then I don't need to do it. I don't think that because you're doing a comedy it need be all ha-ha giggle, because some of the funniest instances in life come out of very serious situations, sometimes sad situations. And that's the relief laughter I feel the world needs. But just for the sake of laughing, and by the time you get home you don't know why—I think there's quite enough of that going on; they don't need me to further that. To change it into something meaningless for the sake of a laugh was a bit of a sore spot to me. It depressed me.
>
> (Margulies 1977)

It seemed that J. J. was too good for ratings to be toned down. Walker, with his background in stand-up comedy, played his character for laughs in a very different way than those who were stage-trained or experienced. John Amos noted Walker's comic skill, particularly his physical comedic skills; he was not untalented. While it was certainly a trope of the show that the Evans family would not really ever catch a break—if they were to leave Cabrini-Green, would there still be a show?—the shift away from some of the significant issues that the show engaged in the first two seasons is gradual. There continue to be references to contemporary social and political issues, such as gas and grocery prices (in other words, the inflation that plagued the country in the mid- to late 1970s) but some of the material that we might mark as explicitly taking up Black issues recedes. It's an important point here to remember that when she landed on Norman Lear's radar, Esther Rolle was already an accomplished actor who had a significant career with one of the most prominent Black theatre troupes in the United States during the 1960s and 1970s. Her stage prominence was what caught Norman Lear's attention when he was looking for someone to cast as Maude's maid. In that role, she would resist playing the same old kind of Black maid because she was well aware of the history of the representation of Black women as maids in theatre, film, and television; "concerned about playing into degrading stereotypes associated with black domestics, Rolle agreed to the part only if she was granted artistic freedom and could develop the character in a non-traditional way" (Chism 2005).

The showrunners were loath to give up their apparent "cash cow" in the character of J. J. and declined Rolle's request to shift the show away from the stereotype that Walker embodied in J. J. Rolle gave them an ultimatum: Walker or me. They chose Walker, and Rolle's character spent the fourth season off in Arizona with new husband Carl. With Rolle gone, Ja'Net Du Bois (Willona) took on a lead role in the series, along with Walker. Season 5 also saw the addition of Janet Jackson as Penny, whom Willona adopts over the course of the season. The show featured story lines involving J. J.'s various schemes and tribulations, and Willona's adoption of Penny. Ultimately, the producers' gamble on J. J. and the addition of Penny was a losing one for them. The inclusion of Janet Jackson did not offset the show's decline in viewership that accompanied the departures of Amos and Rolle. In the 1977–8 season (season 5), the show drops out of the top-rated Nielsen ratings, never to return. As Chism notes, "Rolle and her costar John Amos joined a number of black organizations in criticizing the character development of the eldest son, J. J., played by Jimmie Walker" (Chism 2005). Pressure from the NAACP and other civil rights organizations was also a factor in the demise of both *The Beulah Show* and *Julia*. This underscores the tension between the types of programs and representations that Black audiences want to see, and the competition for white viewers who bring advertising dollars and are accustomed to representations of Blackness that coincide with concepts of Blackness in the white imaginary.

One More Time: Florida Returns

The demise of *Good Times* comes quickly after Rolle's departure. The show is not the same without the influence of both the characters James and Florida, and the actors Amos and Rolle. While Amos never looked back—killing him off meant there was no possibility of his return, and his success playing Kunta Kinte in *Roots* gave him other opportunities—Florida's extended trip to Arizona with Carl could potentially be reversed, and she could return to Chicago. Rolle was working and not inclined to look back or to return to *Good Times*. The show took a nose dive in ratings during the fifth season, and the network could see that relying on the character of J. J., even interspersed with some interesting plots with Willona and Penny, would not rescue the show: "'We felt we had to do something drastic. We had lost the essence of the show,' said Steve Mills, vice president of program production at CBS. 'Without parental guidance the show had slipped. Everything told us that: our mail, our phone calls, our research.

We felt we had to go back to basics'" (Margulies 1978). Rolle could dictate the circumstances under which she would return, and those included making J. J. a more "positive" character. An example of this would be s6:E7, "J. J. the Teacher," in which J. J. teaches painting classes and ends up helping a student who is being abused at home.

The other major change included the return of Norman Paul as executive producer; he had worked on early seasons but left to produce *One Day at a Time*. For Paul, the show had lost its rudder in losing its original sense of family. As Margulies wrote, "the original concept of the Evanses as a poor, struggling ghetto family has been lost, [Paul] believes, and he wants to put greater emphasis on that theme so they aren't simply another version of the middle-class Jeffersons" (Margulies 1978). Indeed, in the final season, both Florida and J. J. would struggle with work (Florida takes a job as a school bus driver).

The final episode of the series does finally move the Evanses and their closest friend out of the ghetto, neatly tying up various story lines. At the beginning of the season, Thelma marries Keith, a professional football player; except during the wedding, he trips and injures his knee, which ends his career as a running back. Throughout the season, Florida, Keith, and J. J. work to keep the family afloat, and the show takes up various issues (teen pregnancy, difficulties for Black people in getting home loans, and addiction). In spite of Rolle's return, however, the show had lost too much audience, and other programs emerged that would draw viewership away from *Good Times*, which moved from a mid-week spot on Wednesday to a spot on Saturday night; Saturdays are considered a death knell for weekly shows, since fewer people watch television regularly on Saturday nights. Keith recovers from his injury sufficiently to get a contract with the Chicago Bears, and a $60,000 salary—sufficient for him to move Thelma and her mother out of the projects. Willona also moves; she is promoted to manager of the boutique, which comes with enough salary to move out as well (she will be downstairs from the Evanses). J. J. sells a cartoon strip and can now afford his own place, and Michael will move on campus in college.

Steps Forward and Back

These are some of the contradictions of *Good Times*; on the one hand, the show valorizes the determination of Black people to survive in the face of structural racism and brought some modicum of Black culture to the majority-white viewership of primetime television in the 1970s. On the other hand, the show also reflects the dominant white supremacist culture that laughs in the face of Black access to the "American Dream," that asserts that "ghetto" life is livable and not as detrimental as the times might show them to be. The show, after all, premiered a mere five years after the killings of Black Panthers Fred Hampton and Mark Clark in Chicago, and only six years after the 1968 riots following the assassination of Dr. Martin Luther King Jr.

Once again, the skilled acting and storied career of a Black woman stage actor pushes for the development of a television program that will depict Black life as livable, complex, and complicated. Rolle's insistence on the focus of Florida's home life, rather than her work as a maid (from her character's introduction on *Maude*, from which they ultimately departed in the development of *Good Times*), with a loving husband and father, was a significant step in the right direction. *Good Times* had great promise. The combination of Monte as creator and Rolle and Amos as significant influences should have produced a program that was a departure from programs that merely recreated the stereotyped roles that had been rooted in the white imaginary since the days of the nineteenth-century Blackface minstrel shows. But this kind of programming could only hold for so long before those old images reasserted themselves in the name of "popularity" and advertising dollars, this time in the figure of Jimmie Walker. And as in previous decades, Black audiences began to tune out when the show reasserted those stereotypes. After three decades, it seems that the ability for *actors* specifically to make significant changes in representations of Black people in general, and Black women in particular, would always be limited. The executives at CBS realized too late that in spite of the popularity of other programming that played to similar stereotypes (*Sanford and Son* and *The Jeffersons*), Black audiences would continue to agitate for different representations of Blackness. The challenge would be convincing television executives that there would be an audience for more diverse representations of Blackness on television, but when writers, directors, and producers could not imagine other kinds of Blackness, such representations would be difficult to find. What would change this in the next decade will be the increasing numbers of Black artists behind the camera, where many of these artistic decisions are made.

As a bit of an addendum, *Good Times* was among the programs that was "recreated" in front of a live audience as part of a kind of tribute to Normal Lear in 2019. The first of these hour-long recreations included *All in the*

Family and *The Jeffersons*, in the spring of 2019, while the second recreated *Good Times* instead. The recreation of "The Politicians," season 3, episode 9 (the one in which James comes into conflict with the family over his support of an older, entrenched politician) starred Viola Davis as Florida. A deeper discussion of the episode, and its importance to this project, can be found in the concluding chapter.

Creating a "Different World" in Television: Black Women Showrunners in the 1990s

As we have seen, in the decades since the 1950s, television has witnessed a gradual increase in the representations of Black people, and particularly Black women. Such representations were limited in the early years of television and tended to fall into two broad categories. First, there were the programs that featured the maid/mammy/jezebel/sapphire of the white imagination—the 1950s *The Beulah Show* was the first of these. These were the programs often protested by the NAACP as "damaging to the growing movement for racial integration" (Hunt 2005), particularly in their reliance on stereotypes that constructed Black people as exclusively poor and working class, denizens of urban ghettos. Even when there was early nominal support for the program, such as with *Good Times*, television's reliance on perpetuating particular images of Black people eventually led to resistance from Black viewers. And even when the program tried to feature a different class of Black people, such as *The Jeffersons*, the ways in which Black people were portrayed remained rooted in the old stereotypes. Because they operated within the confines of the white imagination (brought to life primarily by white writers and producers), they were also at least moderately popular with majority-white audiences.

Second, there were the programs that ended up often being protested by both Black and white audiences, mostly because of the belief that they were "unrealistic" portrayals of African Americans. These programs, like the 1960s series *Julia,* and the extremely popular *The Cosby Show* in the 1980s, portrayed Black people, and particularly Black women, as professionals (a nurse and a lawyer, in the persons of Julia and Claire). Professional Black women, it seemed, were not realistic, nor were Black families that lived middle-class lives. The challenge, of course, was that in creating these representations of a Black middle class, in *Julia* the show's creator and producers placed their Black middle-class "family" in an essentially white neighborhood, and *Cosby's* producers and writers seemed to be embracing a "color-blind," assimilationist narrative, at least to some audiences.[1] The notion that middle-class Black people did not exist, or were so few in number as to be insignificant, was one that persists. In addition, Black critics felt that the representation of middle-class Blacks functioned as a denial of structural racism, and could lead to some (especially whites) blaming poor Blacks for their poverty, especially in the "bootstrap" Reagan era. This type of programming also led to the notion that "authentic" Blackness was necessarily poor or working-class and urban, and any other kind of Blackness was either assimilationist or inauthentic or both (Gray 2005). This, even while Black people and organizations protested the persistent representations of Black people in working-class professions, demonstrates the complicated nature of representing Blackness on television. The tension between representing Blacks as "respectable" and not significantly different from whites, versus representing Black verisimilitude with representations of Black struggles and challenges as well as successes, remains in this era.

The 1980s saw a number of Black-themed television programs that increasingly tried to diversify the types of Black characters that populated network television. As Herman Gray notes, "In black-oriented situation comedies of the late 1970s and early 1980s, especially the long-running *The Jeffersons,* as well as *Benson, Webster, Diff'rent Strokes,* and *Gimmie a Break*, black upward social mobility and middle-class affluence replaced black urban poverty as both setting and theme" (2005, 161). Indeed, the Black characters that populated the programs during this period, while ostensibly different in class from those of earlier periods, remained "surrogate managers, nurturers, and objects of white middle-class fascination" (161).

This decade, and the general acceptance of larger audiences of programming that featured Black families, allowed for what would develop in the 1990s, when we would see a record thirty-seven Black-themed programs, thirty-three of which were sitcoms (Hunt 2005). It is significant that this rise in Black-themed programming is connected to, and in part the result of, the end of the era of the Big Three networks (plus PBS). The development of Fox into a major network in the mid-1980s opened up options for programming specifically aimed at Black audiences. As Zook explains, because "working-class African American and Latino audiences in general did not yet have access to these new technologies [cable subscriptions and videocassette recorders], they continued to rely on the 'free' networks—NBC, CBS, and ABC. Consequently, 'urban' audiences suddenly became a key demographic in the overall network viewership" (Zook

1999, 3). NBC's Black-themed lineup included *The Cosby Show, A Different World*, and *The Fresh Prince of Bel Air*. These programs enjoyed strong ratings through most of their runs, and were a block of programs that proved the appeal of Black programming to larger audiences. Cosby was the number-one Nielsen rated show from 1985–6 to 1989–90. *A Different World* would be in the top of the ratings 1987–8 (ranked second), 1988–9 (third), 1989–90 (fourth), 1990–1 (fourth), and 1991–2 (seventeenth). While *Fresh Prince* did not enjoy ratings quite as high, it still made the top-thirty Nielsen list from 1991–2 to 1993–4 (Brooks and Marsh 2007). Zook argues that this Black-themed lineup would function as a kind of prototype for Fox's development. When Fox emerged on the television scene in 1986, its focus was, to some extent, on Black viewership ("narrowcasting," targeting specific audiences with programming, which also allowed networks to attract specific sponsors who targeted Black and brown urban communities). "By 1993, the fourth network was airing the largest single crop of black-produced shows in television history. And by 1995 black Americans (some 12 percent of the total US population) were a striking 25 percent of Fox's market" (Zook 1999, 4). In the mid-1990s, UPN and WB (Warner Brothers) channels would emerge on basic cable, and they would both model their lineups after Fox, with a significant body of programming devoted to Black-themed programming. By 1995, these three networks and the expansion of basic cable would inaugurate the postnetwork era in television.[2]

In such an environment, the development of Black talent behind the camera would be significant. In spite of this burgeoning of Black programming, the numbers of Black *women* featured in television did not increase significantly; the vast majority of these programs were about Black men, where Black women had less-significant roles. Three programs would develop during the 1990s television boom and would continue into the 2000s that would mark a significant shift in the development of diversity of representations of Black women. These three programs I mark as important here because of what they created for representation of Black women and how they would ground the continuing and dramatic shifts that mark the 2010s: *A Different World,* which was a spin-off from *The Cosby Show; Living Single,* which featured Kim Fields, who had been one of the ensemble in *The Facts of Life* and Queen Latifah, who was coming off of success in both music and film; and *Moesha,* which starred R&B star Brandy and featured Mara Brock Akil as a writer and producer. This chapter focuses on *A Different World* and *Living Single*; in the next chapter, I will deal more significantly with Mara Brock Akil, who has remained a significant content creator in the 2000s and 2010s. Through biographical materials, interviews and other articles on the programs and their creators, and analysis of program episodes, this chapter examines the contributions of the producers and influential actors of these programs to the development of Black verisimilitude and a reshaping of Black representation on television.

In this chapter I will primarily deal with *Different World* and *Living Single*. *A Different World* ultimately functioned as a developmental incubator for Black women working in television production; Debbie Allen's sense of responsibility for mentoring the next generation of Black women writers, directors, and producers facilitated the subsequent increase in experienced Black women showrunners in this decade and beyond. In addition, *Living Single* came with significant star power from Queen Latifah, who originally emerged in the music and film industries, which affected the program's presence, plots, and longevity. I will consider each in turn.

Debbie Allen's "Different World"

As with many other Black women who come to wield relative power in the television industry, Debbie Allen came to television with a significant stage career and formal training in the performing arts. Inspired by the musicals she watched on television as a child, Allen would grow up to pursue her education in the arts at Howard University. Like many Black women who pursued the arts as a vocation after college or formal training, Allen would spend several years working in New York theatre, beginning as a chorus member of *Purlie* and eventually landing a starring role in *Sweet Charity* in 1986, where she was under the direction of Bob Fosse (Post 1993). But before her role in *Sweet Charity*, she would land the role of a teacher in the film version of *Fame* (1980). When the film spun off a television series in 1982, Allen would reprise her role as teacher Lydia Grant. Her work on the show would not be confined to acting; she would direct eleven episodes and win two Emmy awards for choreography. The experience Allen gained during her five years working on *Fame* made her a logical choice when, in 1988 (a year after *Fame* concluded its run), Bill Cosby and Marcy Carsey asked her to take over the direction of *A Different World*.

Different World was a spin-off of *The Cosby Show* and a vehicle for Lisa Bonet. Denise Huxtable ventures off to college at Hillman, an historically Black college where both Cliff and Claire went to college. The first year of the series was directed by Ellen Falcon (Gittelsohn) and produced by Anne Beatts, and the show began as something not quite in line with the aesthetics and culture that existed on *Cosby*. Beatts's previous experience (just before working on *A Different World*, she was the producer for the high school sitcom *Square Pegs*) made her an insider in the world of the situation comedy, but she did not have experience with Black communities or Black colleges. Her vision of *A Different World* was not notably focused on *Black* experiences; instead, the show "revolved around jokes stemming from misunderstandings, pranks and pratfalls, miscued romances, competition, and jealousy" (Coleman and Cavalcante 2013, 34). The show didn't take advantage of its setting—a historically Black college—and critics said the show felt more like high school than college. Minimal plotting put the students in the classroom. There also ended up being an unrealistic racial mixture of students; a young Marisa Tomei was a featured actor, playing Maggie, a white transfer student, and the background students were often a fifty-fifty racial mixture. Critics were not impressed. As a spin-off of *The Cosby Show*, it lacked the racial specificity that grounded *Cosby* and kept it closer to Black communities through regular references to Black culture, such as jazz music, historically Black colleges, and featured cameos by Stevie Wonder, Lena Horne, Sinbad, B. B. King, and Judith Jamison (artistic director of the Alvin Ailey Dance Group), to name just a few. The first season of *A Different World* did not incorporate these kinds of references to a long history of Black culture. The show was also marked by significant discontent among the cast. Even when Sinbad was brought onto the show, Beatts did not want him to bring his particular (and very popular) brand of *Black* comedy to the show. At the end of the first season, the cast was discontented, the critics were unimpressed, and something needed to be done.

Cosby and Carsey decided that the show needed a new direction if it was going to be successful, and asked Allen to take over. Allen was given "a lot of control," which demonstrates the confidence that the production team had in her creative instincts and the direction she would take the show (Hall 1993a). As an alumna of Howard, Allen had a clear sense of what life was like at historically Black colleges; and whatever *A Different World* was at that time, it wasn't like what she remembered. Allen "looked at every past episode of the show … found it silly and decided to make it more relevant, more reflective of a college campus as she had known it—a politically active place against a backdrop of a real community" (B8). This kind of taking-stock and working to make a program more reflective of a community is what Hattie McDaniel did with the radio program of *The Beulah Show*. There, a program focused on Beulah getting her boyfriend to marry her gradually shifted to address issues like college education and careers outside of "maid" for young Black women, and whether a woman could be president. In the 1950s McDaniel had to work against the prevailing notions of what Black women could possibly be. *Good Times,* when it was good, was a domestic comedy that was funny but still took on serious social issues. Allen saw an opportunity to have the comedic elements of the sitcom and also an opportunity to take up more serious issues affecting the Black community (and issues that would be more likely to come up on the campus of an historically Black college). Allen had a significant amount of freedom to reflect the lived experiences of Black people relatively accurately and the position to make those experiences live on the small screen.

Allen relates that "NBC was a little nervous about doing things that were so topical and controversial, and they wanted a show that didn't offend. [...] This was our chance to redefine the logic of the American community in terms of what they see as black" (Hall, B8). Allen begins this work in a television world that had never seen multiple ways of being "authentically" Black in a single space, let alone a program that could highlight Black people and accomplishments in many different fields. Allen began her revision of the program with the visual. She stopped having the young women wear weaves; because Black women's hair has been a marker of a connection to Blackness, incorporating more natural styles created a different aesthetic (just as natural hairstyles were an aesthetic choice on *Good Times*). Allen grew the cast to reflect a diversity of Black womanhood (as well as Black manhood) with actors in a range of sizes and skin tones. Even while somewhat restricted by the format (sitcom) and time slot (primetime but early enough for some younger viewers), Allen managed to make *A Different World* a significant contribution to Black (and US) culture in the 1990s. A program that was still ostensibly about getting through college and working out young romantic relationships also managed to tackle some of the major issues of the period: apartheid, the LA Riots, and HIV/AIDS. So many things were overhauled from the first season, it was nearly a different program (although characters that audiences were growing to love, especially Whitley and Dwayne, remained touchstones). Allen changed the program's introduction; the theme song in the first season was sung by Phoebe Snow, but in the second through fifth seasons it's sung by Aretha Franklin, giving it a very different tone, aesthetically. The final season's theme song was sung by Boyz II Men.

The introductions themselves reveal much about the way the shows are conceptualized. In the first season, the theme song is laid over scenes of pranks, a car wash, Dwayne and Denise dancing in front of a barn (!), Jaleesa jumping double-dutch with two very young-looking girls turning the rope, among others. Aside from the one moment with Dwayne carrying all the women's books, nothing about the intro speaks at all to an historically Black college—or any college, for that matter. The intro doesn't appear to happen on a college campus. Debbie Allen's intro beginning in season 2 is starkly aesthetically different. The intro is cut moving from room to room (as opposed to the random exterior scenes that constituted the intro in the first season). It features members of a marching band; students studying; many different young Black women (who distract a studying Dwayne); football players; Black fraternity and sorority members dancing; a group of uniformed ROTC students; and a final group in their caps and gowns, tossing their mortarboards in a graduation salute. From the first moments of the second season, it is clear we are watching a show that is categorically different from the first season and that we will get a taste of life at an historically Black college. What is so surprising here is that it would have been easy enough for the director and producer to visit an HBCU to get a sense of what it was like on those campuses, so that they could have struck a different tone to the series from the beginning. I wonder if the fact that for so many, *Cosby* seemed racially nonspecific in ways, and that allowed them to think they could construct a show about college students without venturing to college or thinking about the ways in which the HBCU experience was fundamentally different from PWIs. Nevertheless, the new introductions make it clear that this program will be about *college* life, and Allen was dedicated to making it be about things that Black college students—on HBCU and PWI (predominantly white institutions) campuses—were concerned about during the early to mid-1990s.

The overhauled intro prepared the audience for something different when it came to the content of the episodes as well. In the next section, I will discuss some of the plots and important points from the first season of the show.

Season 1: Denise as Square Peg

The first season of *Different World* constitutes Denise's second year at Hillman; her first year happened while she was still a semi-regular on *The Cosby Show*. The season begins with first one, then two new roommates (although it's clear that they intend the room to be a triple, since Denise takes up residence on the top bunk of a bunk bed in the first episode). We are introduced to Jaleesa, who is "older" (twenty-six) and divorced and who will serve (because of her age, neatness, and focus) as a foil for flighty, unserious Denise. While the first episode involves Denise trying out rooming with Whitley, that quickly goes awry, and Denise settles herself with Jaleesa and soon also with Maggie, a white transfer student. The first season is very tied to Denise and to *Cosby*; there are visits by Cliff, Theo, Rudy, Claire, and Denise's grandfather. While many critiques of the first season cite its similarity to the sitcom *Square Pegs* (Mitchell 1988) and its lack of focus on *college* situations and issues, it is not altogether terrible. A few of the programs deal with college issues—for example, Denise's crush on a professor, practicing for and performing on the debate team, and joining the track team with its concomitant practicing. There don't seem to be that many other students. There is too much focus on dorm life; although much of college life is dorm life, we almost never experience the characters in class. The racial mix of the school is startling—there are white extras in every scene (Figure 4). In S1:E14, "Wild Child," Denise helps a working-class young white woman who is smart but not enrolled at Hillman. At one point, Denise says of "Cougar," "She *belongs* here." This episode highlights for me the core problem of the season: the producer and writers have no concept of what Hillman should be like. Their appeal to a diversity that is not present at most HBCUs is vividly on display in this episode.

Figure 4 "Cougar" in class with Denise.

The first season certainly suffered from a lack of narrative through-line and consistency, as well as a lack of specificity that spoke to the history and circumstances of the HBCU. The characters spent a lot of time in two places—the library and café. So while it has a flavor of "college," how that might be different from a small PWI is lost on the production team. As we will see in season 2, Allen tackles the show differently from the first episode.

Making It a Different "Different World"

Allen inherited a show that could not find its way. The obligation to focus on Denise was certainly one thing that held back the production team for season 1; while there was some development of other characters (particularly Whitley and Dwayne, and to a lesser degree, Ron and Jaleesa), the show lacked focus and flitted from one "topic" to the next. The show was primarily focused on dating relationships with a few pseudotopical episodes thrown in (such as the episode that introduced "Cougar"—whom we never see again) and pranks and schemes. The cast was not happy with the way the show was developing, and Lisa Bonet announced to Allen that she was pregnant, having married the previous year. While Bonet and Allen came up with a plot development that could have explained how Denise became pregnant and would have her carry the child to term while a student, Cosby nixed the idea that "Denise Huxtable" would be pregnant and unmarried (Allen 2011). So *A Different World* as a Lisa Bonet vehicle is abandoned, and Allen carries on with some new cast members and embarks on creating something lasting out of what was essentially a star vehicle without its star. While the first season had not been great television, Allen now had to create interest among an audience that was no longer going to watch the show to watch Lisa Bonet. Without any real models for a sitcom focused on college students' experiences, Allen took her task seriously and ultimately created a show that had a significant (six-season) run.

In the first episode, Denise's absence is referenced once, in one sentence from Dwayne, who says he's disappointed that Denise did not return. We quickly become reacquainted with the "old" cast members—Dwayne and Ron discuss being sophomores. When Ron asserts that "the next three years are fat city," and Dwayne comments that "last year was a party compared to what we're in for now. Trust me buddy, you better start taking yourself a little more seriously," it could equally apply to the show, whose new characters (and new aesthetic) will change how audiences feel about the show.

We are introduced to Kim, who is Whitley's new roommate. Kim is a dark-skinned, premed student who is the child of working-class parents and is able to see through Whitley's affect and privilege. She and Whitley immediately clash over Kim's choosing as hers the bed Whitley had slept in the previous year. When Kim implies that something "important" might have happened, Whitley explains that her mother and grandmother, cousin and aunt all slept in that bed. While we know that Whitley has a family legacy at Hillman, this is the first time we get a sense that the college is significantly older, and that its traditions are similar to the kinds of histories and legacies of Ivy League institutions. Again, this consciousness is completely absent (aside from Denise's occasional mentions of her parents meeting at Hillman) in the first season.

The character of Kim brings a more serious focus to the show. In Kim, we get several things. First, Kim embodies the intersections of class, color, and gender. She challenges the audience to accept a primary character who is not wealthy, who is darker skinned, and who is studious. Secondly, her desire to be a physician is further evidence of Allen's take on a show about college—there are students who are attending Hillman with the intention of becoming doctors, lawyers, and activists. While on the one hand this lends verisimilitude to the collegiate environment, it also brings to its audiences something unique. For Black audiences, the representation of a Black college environment provides viewers with the possibility of college. Moreover, Kim is a kind of role model for young women interested in careers in the sciences.

Next, we meet Freddie, Jaleesa's new roommate. Jaleesa now has a short fro, a stark contrast from the longer hair she sported in the first season. Their room is now a double, rather than a triple. Freddie is from New Mexico and about as flighty as Denise. The aesthetics have changed; now, we may see blonde hair, but it is not on white women. The café hang-out is much more crowded, but with only Black people. The first episode, aside from acquainting us with the new cast members, immediately takes up Dwayne's upcoming course with "Dr. War," Colonel Taylor, who is the head of the ROTC (which we never saw in season 1) and a calculus instructor. Then, we meet Walter, who is (now) a graduate student and the dorm director of the men's dorm—another place we never saw in season 1. In fact, we see more young Black men in this first scene than we saw in the entire first season. Their inclusion gives Allen more opportunity to deal with social issues and to represent Black men in college at a time when the number of Black men in college and completing degrees was declining. We deal with Dwayne's imposter syndrome—he feels that although he wants to be an engineer, calculus with Colonel Taylor will expose him as a fraud. Walter meets with Col. Taylor to get Dwayne into his class, insisting that the challenge of working with Col. Taylor will be good for Dwayne. Instead of letting Dwayne slide and take the easy route, Walter tries to ensure Dwayne gets the challenge he needs to be successful in school and in life.

Allen puts a fine point on life at Hillman. What the characters experience in this *Different World* 2.0 is a more fully imagined college life. Their hang-out gets a name (The Pit) and a cantankerous cook, Vernon Gaines, played by Lou Myers. They get a homecoming football game against Hampton, a mention of Morehouse; they get a homecoming step show (Figure 5). The oldest living graduate comes for homecoming; she is idolized by Whitley, and her Black bourgeois credit is affirmed by the mention of her being a member of the Links.[3] Football games, pick-up basketball games (which comes from having a more fully realized male presence in the show), and baseball populate the show. In class, students study logic and debate Kant in philosophy class. The tone of the show is different, more serious. Students study at the library—they don't just go there to pick up dates. Fraternity and sorority sweatshirts begin to show up, along with the Hillman seal on sweatshirts. Hillman even has a motto: *Deus Nondum Te Confecit* (God has not yet finished). Now, the entire cast, including named extras, is Black. Allen even created a context for Hillman, including a "history" of the school, so that episodes could remain true to the created location, an amalgam of several different HBCUs. It became "a complex and dynamic show reflecting a diverse set of [black] characters and a broad range of often competing viewpoints concerning pressing social issues and struggles" (Coleman and Cavalcante 2013, 39).

Figure 5 Hillman Step Show.

It was also vitally important to Allen that the show reflect not only the Black diversity (class, skin color, and ideologies) of historically Black colleges but also their long history with social activism and taking up of social issues (Allen 2011). One of the key changes in having a Black woman at the helm of this program is not just what it accomplishes in terms of the representations of Black women, but really of Black people as a whole. In what follows, we will examine several of the episodes from seasons two to six that take up social issues.

Taking on Social Issues

One of the most significant things about Allen's production of *Different World* is her insistence on making Hillman look like the HBCU with which she was familiar, asserting the social justice emphasis of many of the students on HBCU campuses. And while Allen's experience at Howard is not universal to every HBCU, the current of activism and social justice is prominent there. This is also a more pointed divergence from the *Cosby* era; while Black culture (albeit middle-class Black culture) suffused the Huxtable household in many ways, Allen chose to draw on Black cultures in more explicit ways. In what follows, I choose some representative programs from several seasons that are sharply focused on broader social issues. This is not to say that these are typical episodes of the program; indeed, many of the episodes focus on more quotidian college issues, such as succeeding in classes, dating, and other social relationships. However, because of the social justice aspect of life at many HBCUs, Allen emphasized these in her interviews and discussions of the show. For our purposes, they are significant because they successfully address these social issues head-on, in ways that *Good Times* had tried to do.

In season 2, episode 20, "No Means No," Dwayne has concerns about the baseball player on whom Freddie has a crush. In a conversation with Dwayne, Garth talks about his history with women, especially his belief that sometimes, they need "convincing" to have sex. Dwayne tries to keep Freddie from going on a date with Garth but is unsuccessful. Dwayne has a conversation with Walter in which he questions Garth's philosophy. Walter convinces Dwayne that what Garth is describing is rape. A discussion of rape, specifically date rape and rape culture *among men*, is a significant conversation and one that I believe is an important contribution. Within the discussion between Dwayne and Walter, there are specific references to Black culture (specifically music). The way that both men demonstrate an ethic of care toward the women in their community is also notable. It is but one example of how Allen's philosophy and her vision of the show as one that would address contemporary issues made an impact.

This episode is from 1989, Allen's first season with the show. It has clearly moved away from the lighter topics of the first season to the characters who would come to define the show—Freddie, Kim, Whitley, Dwayne, Walter, and Jaleesa. Dwayne rescues Freddie from being assaulted in Garth's car, and they turn him into the police; they also get the young woman who was raped by Garth to give her story to the police. At moments, the show reads like a PSA—in the opening credits with a statement about the nature of the episode, and when Lettie explains how difficult date rape cases can be to prosecute, for example. But Freddie is able to count on her friends, including Dwayne, in her hour of need.

The episode, "A World Alike" (s3:e16), engages with the challenges surrounding the antiapartheid movement and the responding call for institutions and businesses to divest from South Africa. The official US government policy was "constructive engagement," but there was a significant movement centered on divestment that was largely supported by Black activists in South Africa. A key element of the divestment movement was college students pushing their academic institutions to divest. It should not surprise us that Allen and the writers of *A Different World* would take up this issue as well, and that they would take it up in all of its complexity. An upper middle-class transfer student, Julian, meets Whitley, who immediately falls for him. He is part of the student antiapartheid movement on Hillman's campus, a group of which Freddie is also an integral part. Freddie's job is to comb through the university's investments to find those that are still invested in South Africa. A key one—Orange Glow Soda—was supposed to have divested but hasn't. Hillman is also heavily supported by Orange Glow, from funding the engineering lab that Dwayne is part of, to funding scholarships to premed students like Kim—who happens to get one of these scholarships just as Orange Glow's deception is discovered.

Whitley is all for divestment, of course, until she realizes that Kim's scholarship is from Orange Glow. Whitley is not always the kindest person, and we don't necessarily think that she likes Kim, but this episode reveals there is more to Whitley than her upper-middle-class snobbery. She encourages Kim to keep the scholarship in spite of the problems; without the scholarship, because of her father's ill health (covered in a previous episode), Kim will have to work two jobs in order to stay at Hillman. Here is another example of how Allen kept important plot points from episode to episode; it presumes that viewers follow the show, certainly, but it also attests to a kind of seriousness and dedication on the part of Allen to make the show "work." While many sitcoms may not keep this level of detail and consistency across programs, Allen does so in this program, and such connection and history becomes more common among sitcoms; we see this in shows like *Black/ish* in the mid-2010s. First, a look at a dialogue between Whitley and Julian:

> J: I hope the school shows the same sense of responsibility when we ask them to cut their financial ties with Orange Glow soda.
> W: When you say "cut financial ties," you don't mean scholarships ...
> J: I mean everything.
> W: But Julian, my roommate was just awarded a scholarship from Orange Glow.
> J: I'm sorry.
> W: I can count on you?
> J: What for?
> W: Not to ask the students to give their scholarships back! Least not til Kimmie cashes her lil check.
> J: Whitley, I sympathize with your roommate's situation, but I can't do that.
> W: Why not?
> J: Because we can't accept money from a company that supports a system based on racial segregation and exploitation.
> W: Kim didn't create apartheid, why should she have to suffer?
> J: Because she has responsibility, we all do, to the brothers and the sisters in South Africa.
> W: I don't even know them! I know Kim!
> J: How can you be so short-sighted?
> W: And what grand sacrifice have you made, Julian? Have you given up a scholarship?
> J: You are completely missing the point.
> W: Au contraire, I think I've hit it. You see I'm not on financial aid either, but I don't go around dictating the social responsibilities of those who are.
> J: That's not what I'm doing.
> W: Sounds like it to me.
> J: Because you're not listening.
> W: Because you're blowing more hot air than a bellows.
> J: If you'd think about it, you'd realize that I'm right.
> W: No I won't.

Shortly after their encounter, we venture to the student meeting about divestment. Featured are two students who are at Hillman from South Africa. Here, Allen and her writers dive into the complexity of how Black people in the United States might engage with the antiapartheid struggles in South Africa:

> Kobe: I support divestment. But I don't think any Hillman student should give up their scholarship to achieve it. […] My education here is being funded by the factory in which my father has toiled all his life for seventeen cents an hour. And once I complete my studies, I intend to go back home to carry on the struggle.
>
> Mbubunni: But I can never go home. At thirteen I was arrested for participating in the student protests in Soweto. Many of my friends died in those protests. We may not agree on how to address the problem, but we must agree to do something.
>
> Julian: Kobe, if we Americans use Orange Glow's blood money, how do the people of South Africa benefit?
>
> Kobe: By the example of your triumph. When you grow up in a South African township, all you see is poverty, and disease. You eat rotten food, you breathe foul air—then you see the white suburb, the air is clean, the houses so beautiful, you begin to ask yourself, why is it so? The only logical answer seems to be that as a black person, squalor and shame are all that you deserve because you're by nature inferior.
>
> Whitley: Don't you know any black people who live decently?
>
> Kobe: Whitley, see, you cannot even conceive of it. When I came here, I could not even conceive of people like you. […] Here, I learned that the way that it is, is not the way that it has to be.

In the end, Kim decides not to accept the scholarship; she says that she couldn't live with herself knowing that she took money from Orange Glow. The students decide that they will work with Orange Glow to set up a timetable for them to divest. The episode strikes me as a stark contrast from the way that the HBCU was conceptualized in the first season; this diversity of Blackness, across class and nation, was not the diversity of the first season. The absence of students from the African continent was starkly inconsistent with the actual enrollments of historically Black colleges.

Several episodes from season 4 highlight domestic issues. Episode 3, "Blues for Nobody's Child," has Freddie working with children in the foster care system, learning about how difficult it is for Black children, especially older children, to be adopted. On the surface, Freddie is flighty, but we see that she is quite smart and very dedicated to her studies and to the causes she cares about. She shames one of her professors into thinking about adopting the young boy who can't seem to find a family, and eventually, he adopts the boy. In the introduction, this professor tells the children a story about Amistad; later in the episode, Ron discusses W. E. B. Du Bois in class. In episode 8, "Love thy Neighbor," Ron is featured after he disparages homeless people during one of his classes. He encounters a homeless man he quickly recognizes as the former owner of Ray Nay's BBQ. Ron learns a lot about some of the causes of homelessness; Ray sold his restaurant to take care of his elderly mother, and her medical bills bankrupted him. At seventy years old, he doesn't want to go back into the restaurant business, no matter how much Ron thinks he should. Colonel Taylor is the central character in episode 10, "The Apple Doesn't Fall." Invited to join a country club, Shade Falls, which has a long history of segregation, Col. Taylor is surprised that just about everyone, from his son to Vernon Gaines, thinks the club only wants him as a token, and that they will largely remain segregated once he has been admitted. Gaines's father was a caddy there, and Gaines declines even the invitation to golf there as Taylor's guest. When Taylor has the club president over, he realizes that this baby step toward integration is all about getting a PGA championship at the club (the PGA would not grant a championship match to a segregated club). He doubts the sincerity of the desire to integrate, and decides not to join the club after all.

One of the most important (and impactful) of the season 4 episodes is episode 23, "If I Should Die Before I … " With Whoopi Goldberg as Dr. Jordan, a public speaking professor, Allen takes up the issue of HIV. Of all the episodes of season 4, it is the most "controversial," since it deals with sexuality. Tisha Campbell plays Josie Webb, a shy student in the public speaking class. Dr. Jordan works to bring Josie out of her shell, encouraging her to look at the audience instead of down at her feet. To get Josie and the whole class more engaged, she gives them an assignment to write their own eulogies. Predictably, Whitley's is too long, and Dwayne's doesn't mention Whitley. But Josie decided to use the moment as an opportunity to reveal her HIV status and her reckoning with her own mortality. The context of the classroom enables Dr. Jordan to make the revelation a larger learning moment for the rest of the students. Some react with horror (one student says she is going to request to change dorms, since Josie lives down the hall from her), but reliably Kim (the premed student, of course) is there to support Josie and to put to rest some of the rumors and misinformation about HIV. While looking at this episode in 2019 is slightly cringe-worthy—we know significantly more about HIV now than we did then—the episode is commendable for engaging heterosexual transmission among young Black people, who remain a significant at-risk group even now.

Allen did what she set out to do. Certainly, she rescued a program that was on the verge of being a disaster and made it sing as part of NBC's Thursday night lineup. The episode on HIV was the highest rated episode for its week, in spite of advertisers pulling out and much resistance from the network (Allen 2011). In the face of pushback on many of the socially relevant episodes, Allen persisted and created one of the most relevant shows on television in the 1990s. In addition to the show's success, Allen made waves in another way; she mentored several young Black women who worked in production on the show, gaining valuable experience that would allow them to enter into the ranks of television's Black showrunners.

Yvette Lee Bowser Takes on Living Single

One of the people who worked on *A Different World* was Yvette Lee Bowser. She began on the program as a production assistant and program consultant, then as a writer, and eventually moved up to produce in the 1991–2 season (25 episodes, credited as Yvette Denise Lee). With the conclusion of *A Different World*, a new opportunity opened up. Both Kim Fields and Queen Latifah had "holding deals" with Warner Brothers, which would become the show's production company (although the show would be broadcast on Fox).[4] They "urged the studio to meet with at least one black woman writer," and out of that process, Bowser was hired (Zook 1999, 66). With the new, diverse depictions of Blackness and Black issues that Allen created in *A Different World*, Bowser was able to take advantage of audiences' familiarity with multiple kinds of Blackness and Black womanhood. She created a program that focused on the lives of four Black women friends who share a brownstone in Brooklyn. In a way, Khadijah, Synclaire, Max, and Regine are the "next step" up from the college friends of *A Different World*; Bowser discussed them as different aspects of herself. While the final season of *A Different World* took up the postcollege lives of some of the characters, it was still rooted in the college experience. Audiences were hungry for a program to follow up on *Different World*, one in which Black women figured prominently. (A brief look into the sitcoms of the 1990s shows that aside from *Thea* and *Moesha*, the programs were dominated by stories about men—*Martin, In the House, The*

Wayans Brothers, Malcom & Eddie, The Jamie Foxx Show, The Steve Harvey Show, Goode Behavior, Cosby, Smart Guy, Between Brothers, Arsenio Hall, The Hughleys, and *The Parkers.*) *Living Single* was unique in showing relationships between professional Black women, which will set the stage for future programming that also could take up the lives of Black professional women. The show highlighted the variety of Black women, with the types of well-rounded characters that often elude other programs. They are still young, at the early stages of their careers, and still finding their way in the world. They mark a "next step" from *A Different World,* away from the academic realm. Those who were going to graduate or professional school have done that (Max and Kyle). We see both interior and exterior lives of the women; we see them at work, and we see them at home. Their mix of professional lives—lawyer, magazine editor, and actor among them— shows a side of incipient Black middle-class life separate from the "black lady" presence of characters like Claire Huxtable (Thompson 2009). Bowser's young Black women are not confined to the "proper" sexuality, and in fact the series, which focuses on the professional and dating lives of the characters, allows for sexuality outside of marriage.

That Bowser put young, single Black women in the center of a sitcom was fairly radical for the time (in all honesty, it's still somewhat radical). First, Bowser's characters are decidedly emerging into the middle-class; they do so, however, without necessarily having middle-class parents to fall back on (in one episode, Khadijah needs money to keep her magazine afloat, and there's no discussion of her asking her parents for money). Their cohousing arrangement is also evidence of their emerging status; as young urban professionals, they still do not have the financial stability to live entirely on their own. Bowser is showing the first postintegration generation coming of age, still rooted in Black community and experience. The friends live in Brooklyn, very much pregentrification. The women of the show are also a departure from the "ladies" of earlier programs, including *Cosby.* Here, again, I think *Different World,* with its open embrace of young Black people's sexuality in many of its episodes, provided a context and prepared the television audience for something other than the understated sexuality of the married Black woman. These representations begin to challenge "respectability politics" that used "positive" stereotypes designed to combat the sexualization of Black women in television and film. As Zook notes, some of this was not by Bowser's design but rather the network's desire to capture the buzz around Terry McMillan's *Waiting to Exhale*; "the show went from being a slice-of-life comedy about girlfriends to a narrative about the 'male quest,' or the

'Fight for Mr. Right' as one two-part episode was dubbed" (1999, 67). While the network may have had McMillan's novel in mind, Bowser's work is significantly of a younger generation than the women of McMillan's novel.

It is worth noting that despite that buzz and the show's similarity to *Friends*, *Living Single*, with its Black cast and its home on Fox, never had the ratings or the longevity of *Friends* (which it preceded by a year). In an interview with the web magazine *Shadow and Act*, Erika Alexander argues that the fact of their Blackness doomed *Living Single* to a television "ghetto" (Obie 2019). A contrast between the two programs also reveals stark differences between Black and white representations, and Black and white realities. The Black twenty-somethings are (except for Max's period of unemployment) mostly professionally employed—magazine editor, wedding planner, lawyer—where the Manhattan-based *Friends* have significantly fewer professional positions for the most part (Mock 2017). The program has also been compared to HBO's *Sex and the City*; it has been argued that *Living Single* was a "blueprint" for HBO's series (Viera 2013). As Viera notes, the character types from *Living Single* are echoed in *Sex and the City*. That *Living Single*'s influence on the television landscape remains largely invisible would reveal Alexander's critique to be accurate.

It is also important that *Living Single* emerges onto television at the same time that hip-hop takes off in popular culture. Hip-hop's aesthetics—particularly among women hip-hop artists like Queen Latifah—would openly embrace sexuality in a rejection of the respectability politics that dominated the 1980s. We might look to the iconic groups Salt-n-Pepa and TLC, as well as the show's own Queen Latifah, as exemplifying this open embrace of an assertive Black female sexuality. Songs such as *Let's Talk about Sex, Push It,* and *Waterfalls* are emblematic of the ways that Black female hip-hop artists would embrace sexuality. Perhaps in part because of Queen Latifah's important presence on the show, *Living Single* would embrace the hip-hop aesthetic of the early 1990s and its strong departure from the respectability that surrounded shows like *The Cosby Show*. We see some of this in the characters, and how they are presented to us, and how they interact with each other. We also see this quite literally in Season 3, episode 12, in which TLC guest stars on the program. The plot around their appearance—Overton repeatedly dreams about them after watching their videos before going to bed—is somewhat frivolous, but does have momentary seriousness when Overton asks whether his dreams about the group reveal something about his relationship with Synclaire.

Thus the series was largely concerned with the dating lives of the characters (which is not completely surprising, as the title of the show emphasizes the characters' "single" status). And while it does not always take on the larger social justice issues that Allen did in *A Different World*, the facts of living their lives as Black people in the United States means that issues outside of dating come up even in a program that is focused on heterosexual dating. Through the show's seasons, some episodes took up certain social issues of the time. In season 1, Overton participates in a big brother program, and in a different episode the women fear a burglary after Regine is mugged. Khadijah is threatened with a sexual harassment suit by a male employee, and at the end of the first season, Max is suspended from her job as a lawyer, and her period of unemployment extends into the second season. When Max finally gets another job, it is not in the same type of role as her first job in a high-powered corporate firm, but as a public defender. While the show does not go into details about the significance of this change for Max, the income potential is especially significant. Max's inability to "fit in" at the big firm, in spite of her distinguished law school resume and passing the bar on her first try, is specifically marked in the episode about not being about either race or gender—when Max is passed over for a job that she thinks she has, we find that the person who was hired was also Black and female. This moment is a curious one, because it seems to recreate a narrative about individuality and "personal responsibility" rather than a moment focused on structural racism. The episodes around Max's suspension and unemployment reflect a sensibility around upward mobility that lays the responsibility for getting (and keeping) those positions squarely on the individual.

In another important episode in season 2, Regine undergoes breast reduction surgery. This episode blends a serious health issue with sharp comedy, mostly focused on Regine's perpetual pursuit of a husband. Regine's doctors recommend breast reduction surgery to alleviate her back pain, but Regine, who sees her own value in her physical attractiveness, is reluctant to go through the procedure. After considering both the health and social effects of the surgery, she decides she will have the surgery after all; however, she immediately regrets her choice. After the surgery, she convinces herself that she is not the same and confirms it to herself by her inability to attract one of Kyle and Overton's friends—while she is dressed in an oversized denim shirt. Kyle helps her to see that her value is in her intelligence, business savvy, and many other elements—not her breast size.

In one more significant episode from season 2, Kyle's locs may keep him from getting a promotion. Kyle works as a stockbroker, and his professional style is one of the comedic contrasts between him and his housemate, Overton. The issue of Black hair emerges at this point in part because of the hip-hop aesthetics of the show; the show normalizes not only a variety of Black women's hairstyles but also that of Black men (through Kyle). During the 1990s, the idea that certain Black hairstyles were not "clean" or "professional" emerged, especially as Blacks moved into positions (like Kyle's job as a stockbroker) that they had not had in decades before. In previous decades, the "logical" solution would have been for Kyle to cut his hair to a short afro, which was (and to a degree still is) considered an "acceptable" hairstyle for Black men (that, or Overton's shaved head).

In season 3, Max is surprised to find that her college roommate is entering a same-sex marriage. Max has agreed to hold a wedding shower for her friend Shayla and her fiancée Chris. The script uses a gender-neutral name for Shayla's fiancée so that when Chris comes to the door, Max is surprised. Max's resistance to the disclosure is not because of Shayla's sexuality, but because they have been friends for a long time, and Shayla didn't feel like she could tell Max. Things do not improve when Max discovers that Khadijah has known since their junior year in college. The episode is full of moments that range from queer-friendly to queer-positive. When Synclaire claims that she doesn't know any lesbians, Khadijah reminds her of their aunt; Synclaire responds that "Aunt Gladys just never found the right man … like her roommate Aunt Hazel." Kyle is ridiculed for his attempts to talk to the women arriving for the shower. The primary issue for Max is not her friend's sexuality, but that she didn't know; but what she didn't know is that Shayla was in love with her in college. Shayla reveals this in a private moment in the kitchen during the shower. Max is stunned but eventually comes around to maintain their friendship. While the show ultimately focused on romantic plots, it was not devoid of episodes that took on social issues.

Star Power: Queen Latifah and Kim Fields

In a book about Black women that focuses on their "star" power translating to influence as they negotiate the television industry, Queen Latifah's and Kim Fields's influence on the existence of *Living Single* is important. As stated earlier, their deal with Warner Brothers was the impetus for creating the show. Fields came to the show with significant television experience; in particular, her nine years as "Tootie" on the girls' boarding school show *The Facts of Life* had made her well known in the television world. After *Facts* concluded its run in 1988,

Fields did a few guest spots on several programs, including *Fresh Prince of Bel Air*, but was not in a regular series. It was in part through her influence that Warner Brothers considered, and then hired, Yvette Bowser to create and produce *Living Single*. She notably had the writers include as a story line her breast reduction surgery in a moving episode that addresses body issues and self-esteem, particularly for Fields's character Regine. Fields's character on *Living Single* was a significant change from the friendly and naïve Tootie; through this character, Fields was able to expand her acting repertoire and show. She would eventually move into directing and production, and continues to work in the field.

Queen Latifah's presence on the show is also significant. Unlike Fields, who came to the program as a television actor, Latifah came to her "star" power through music and film. Her hip-hop credentials were solid; she was one of the most prominent women in hip-hop at the time. Her debut album, *All Hail the Queen* (Tommy Boy Records, 1989), reached number six on the Billboard Hip-Hop/R&B list and was a gold album. It featured the song *Ladies First*, the lyrics of which make a statement about the presence of women in hip-hop, including the lines

> Some think that we can't flow (can't flow)
> Stereotypes, they got to go (got to go)
> I'm a mess around and flip the scene into reverse
> (With what?) With a little touch of "Ladies First"

As Zook argues, Queen Latifah's persona exists in a kind of "sexual liminality" that signifies a Black feminism; her ability to gender code-switch, from a high femininity to a female masculinity, signifies her as potentially lesbian (1999). Prior to her work on *Living Single*, Latifah had roles in three films—*Jungle Fever*, *House Party 2*, and *Juice*—and had also appeared in two episodes of *Fresh Prince of Bel Air*. In some ways, Latifah's emergence into television reminds me of that of Ethel Waters, who came into acting through her singing career. During the run of *Living Single*, Latifah would go on to release her album *Black Reign* (1993); her song *U.N.I.T.Y.* from that album would win a Grammy award. We can see *U.N.I.T.Y* as an exemplar of Latifah's politics at this point. The song became a kind of hip-hop feminist anthem. In it, she objects to male hip-hop artists referring to Black women as "bitches" and "hoes"; she creates a persona who realizes that she should leave a domestic violence situation and also calls out young women who adopt gangsta personas. Latifah's particular brand of Black feminism appeared from time to time on the show; her brand of "nationalist aesthetics [...] also expressed a certain racial pride, symbolized by books such as *African Americans: Voices of Triumph* and *I Dream a World* strewn across the coffee table, Africanesque statues placed throughout the living room, kente fabrics hanging from a coatrack, and baseball caps reading 'Negro League'" (Zook 1999, 71). Unlike Waters, however, Latifah was instrumental in the show being developed, since it was in part her insistence on Warner interviewing Black women as show developers, and some of its success can be attributed to her popularity and presence on the show (she also sang the theme song).

Mentoring and Moving Ahead

Ultimately, what are among the most important points of this excursion down memory lane is how the television industry changed and how the influence of Black women as "showrunners" made significant changes to the representations of Black women specifically, Black people generally, and Black culture more broadly. There were two things that radically changed television in the 1990s, at least as far as representations of African Americans are concerned. The first of these is the breakup of the primetime monopoly by the Big Three networks (ABC, CBS, and NBC). When we see the numbers of new programming featuring Black people go from nineteen to thirty-seven in a decade, something significant has changed. The decade's three new networks—Fox, WB, and UPN—accounted for twenty-one of that same decade's new "Black" shows. Some of them were terrible, but they got a chance to start. On the Big Three networks, there was not much change. Programs like *In Living Color*, *Martin*, and *Living Single* would help to establish Fox as a major player. This initial proliferation of new opportunities for trying out new programming, and new showrunners and production staff, would continue to expand into the 2000s, where we will see some consolidation in these broadcast channels but watch other cable channels begin their own original programming where once they only showed programs in syndication (TNT, TBS), and original series programming developed on what had been pay movie channels (HBO, Showtime), culminating in original series programming on streaming services (Netflix, Amazon). While it is conceivable that a program like *Living Single* could have a successful run on a Big Three network, the fact that it fit on upstart Fox made it possible for new representations to enter into popular culture. In fact, NBC would see a decrease in Black-themed shows in the post-*Cosby*/*Different World*/*Fresh Prince of Bel Air* era, and the Big Three would focus efforts in other areas, while occasionally including a Black-themed, or Black-starring, sitcom in its primetime offerings.[5]

The second is the importance of both mentoring and example in developing new young talent. Debbie Allen's experience on the *Fame* series gave her opportunities to act and choreograph dance numbers and eventually to direct episodes. That experience, and the respect she was afforded because of her stage career (a theme that I have seen again and again in looking at these broad changes in representation) allowed her to step into a failing program and make it into something that was popular and broke open previously unseen representations of Blackness. Allen's ability to convince (white) network executives to take "chances" on episodes on the LA Riots, date rape, AIDS, and antiapartheid activism, all while representing the previously unrepresented—the historically Black college/university—paved the way for where television representation *could* potentially go. Allen's mentorship of Bowser, who eventually worked up from intern to producer, put someone in place with experience and different ideas about how Blackness could be on television at just the point when television was set to offer new opportunities. Bowser would go on to work on UPN show *Half and Half,* one of the network's core of Black programming until the merger with WB, and would go on to work on other Black-themed programming as a producer, executive producer, or consulting producer on programs such as *Dear White People* and *black-ish*. Writer and producer Mara Brock Akil, who began as an editor and writer for *Moesha,* one of the other 1990s success stories, went on to create *Girlfriends,* which ran for eight seasons on UPN/CW. These women's contributions to Black television paved the way for new possibilities in representations of Black women, and opened up new avenues for Black women showrunners in the decades that would follow.

Twenty-First-Century Black Womanhood

In the first decade of the twenty-first century, not much changes in the world of television in terms of Black representation. The diversification of outlets that we saw in the late 1990s continues to allow for an interesting diversity of television programming featuring Black people and, to some extent, Black stories. For the most part, these will remain relegated to the world of the sitcom and will remain primarily on the "new" channels, particularly UPN, "which alone accounted for an incredible 50 percent of these shows" (Hunt 2005). This has implications for the latter half of the 2000s, when media consolidation would have a significant effect on Black-themed television programming that would last until the latter half of the 2010s. The first decade of the twenty-first century doesn't look significantly different from the last decade of the twentieth century, at least as far as Black representation is concerned. Just one decade later, though, a multiply shifting landscape will open up possibilities for Black women in the industry. This chapter examines the moves and accomplishments of Black women in producer/writer/director roles, focusing on Shonda Rhimes, Mara Brock Akil, Issa Rae, and Ava DuVernay.

The stagnation in the 2000s is not altogether surprising, particularly as the attacks of September 11, 2001, would incline television to take fewer risks amid a more conservative viewership. The relative prosperity of the late 1990s also saw more conservative policies, especially around poverty and crime. The Clinton administration's collaboration with a conservative-dominated Congress saw the passage of "welfare reform," otherwise known as TANF (Temporary Assistance to Needy Families). The image of the welfare recipient continued to be Black, female, and urban, in spite of the actual numbers of welfare users nation-wide. This controlling image continued to impact legislation, and the passage of TANF was supported by many people who blamed generational poverty on "limitless" welfare programs. The institution of a five-year limit for benefits and a work requirement were regressive policies that did nothing to lift people out of poverty.[1] TANF was not the only Civil Rights backlash that would typify the late 1990s. Increasingly draconian drug and criminal justice policies (in light of the "crack epidemic"), especially mandatory minimum sentences for drug offences, would spike the numbers of incarcerated people, particularly Blacks and Latinos (Fellner 2000). This had significant impact on Black communities, especially urban communities, across the country. In the arts, hip-hop would gain a larger audience, particularly in terms of crossover onto pop music charts. As television would move more and more to niche programming ("narrowcasting"), communities would continue to resegregate after decades of more integration.

A New Media Landscape

This more conservative political climate would be heightened with the contested 2000 election of George W. Bush. However this second Bush administration might have governed, the 2001 terror attacks and subsequent wars in Afghanistan and Iraq would significantly change the administration's focus. This era, typified by two wars against "Middle-Eastern Terrorists," would usher in renewed narratives about the meanings of "American" and belonging. In addition to those social and cultural changes, we would see economic changes that would, in the long run, be devastating particularly for people of color, who were hardest hit by the 2008 recession. This renewed wave of conservatism would culminate in a retrenchment in terms of television representation. In the year of the 2000 election (1999–2000), the Big Four (ABC, NBC, CBS, and Fox) would not broadcast a single Black-themed program on the primetime schedule. While Fox had used the labor and talents of several Black-themed shows to increase the network's popularity, it would abandon this once it had established itself, focusing on programming that appealed to "broader" audiences (*The Simpsons, The X Files, Ally McBeal*).

The 1999–2000 season would be a harbinger; Black-themed situation comedy would return in only a limited fashion on the Big Four networks in the years immediately following the 2001 season—only one show on ABC (*My Wife and Kids*), three on Fox (*The Bernie Mac Show, Wanda at Large*, and *Cedric the Entertainer Presents*), and two on NBC (*Whoopi* and *Tracy Morgan Show*). Of the sixteen Black-themed sitcoms that aired between 2000 and 2003, ten were broadcast on either UPN or the WB. In the years between 2004 and 2006 (2004–5 season and 2005–6 season), once again UPN would continue to offer

Black-themed sitcoms as part of its lineup. In the 2004–5 season, UPN had four of the few offered; they would be joined only by *My Wife and Kids* on ABC, *The Bernie Mac Show* on Fox, and the legal drama *Kevin Hill* on UPN. In the 2005–6 season, as UPN and WB began the process of consolidating, UPN would add *Everybody Hates Chris* while cancelling *Eve, Half and Half,* and *One on One.* In the fall of 2006, there would still be only four Black-themed programs on the new CW; in the meantime, network television would content itself with reality programming and new additions to the successful procedural series and ensemble programs that dominated the Nielsen ratings. In 2008, the writer's strike would disrupt programming in favor of more unscripted "reality" shows. Even while there were more cable outlets, many were associated with the same networks (F/X, for example, was a Fox channel). The merger of Disney and ABC in 1996 represents one example of media consolidation; thus even while there were more *channels* on cable television, they were owned by fewer and fewer companies. While this trend began in the 1990s, it would accelerate during the 2000s.

Even while there were more outlets, that increase in television and cable outlets did not necessarily translate into more Black-themed programming. The persistence of the networks' aversion to Black-themed content would continue, and in spite of "proof" (i.e., ratings) of broader appeal of Black-themed programming to mainstream audiences, networks would continue to be wary of investing in new, "risky" programming. This is evident in the programming in the 2000s, where television's "diversity" remained only in the ensemble procedurals (*Without a Trace, CSI,* the *Law and Order* franchise, etc.) and perhaps typified by Shonda Rhimes's *Grey's Anatomy,* which we will take up below. What Maryann Erigha discusses about the racial politics of the movie industry is also applicable to television; shows (or films, in Erigha's work) that have a Black lead or focus on Black people are presumed to only appeal to Black audiences, and it is economically risky to invest much in them: "What transpires is a self-fulfilling prophecy: raced marketing plans reinforce the perception that Black movies are unbankable to non-Black audiences" (2019, 55). Networks are similarly reluctant to invest in too much programming that will appeal to "niche" audiences. After all, advertising dollars are the lifeblood of television, and advertisers want the largest possible audiences for their products. Programs with a smaller or a "niche" audience ultimately don't make enough money, and networks can only "afford" so many of those.

Networks and advertisers grew concerned about audience viewing habits, especially around viewers watching commercials, with the advent of videocassette recording in the 1980s. This intensified as the presence of new technologies emerged in the 2000s. Digital video recording emerged in 1999, with TiVo debuting at the Consumer Electronics Show that year. The DVR would be the first of the emerging technologies that shifted how audiences watch programming. It enabled easy set up of automatically recording programs that could be watched at a later time. The DVR also allows audiences to watch one program while recording another and to skip through commercials. While time slots did not become irrelevant, audiences could save programs to watch at different times than they were broadcast.

Of course, the DVR is only one of the many factors that shifted television and viewing habits in the first decade of the twenty-first century, whose early years brought three additional technological developments into the world of the televisual that helped to shift how people consumed "television." They are deeply connected to each other. The primary of these is advances in Internet technology that brought broadband, high-speed Internet to households. The accessibility of high-speed data, combined with the development of Web 2.0 (interactivity with websites and programming that enhanced the development of *social* media), opened up new options for the distribution of content. Secondly, smartphones and small digital video cameras would enable users to more easily create content, including video, and upload it to social media sites. Thirdly, video editing software would become cheaper and therefore more available to enable creating more professional-looking videos. And the presentation of user-created content on sites like MySpace (and later YouTube, Facebook, Twitter, Tumblr, etc.) paved the way for the most recent advance in technology in the televisual realm: streaming media.

I view the advent of streaming media much like the expansion of cable television outlets in the mid- to late 1990s. Clearly, the data showed in that instance that the proliferation of outlets for television programming across basic cable networks significantly increased, even if only temporarily, the programming that focused on or featured African American stories. It is also true that many of them continued to deploy the familiar stereotypes or types of Blackness seen in previous eras; there was some innovation, as we saw with *Living Single* and some other programs, but even those additional networks were still owned and controlled by an ever-shrinking number of companies, as mergers created media monopolies. Most outlets, however varied their programming, are ultimately the properties of one of eight companies: Comcast (NBC Universal), Disney (ABC and a variety of other outlets like A&E and

ESPN), 21st Century Fox, Time Warner (HBO), National Amusement (CBS, Viacom, etc.), E. W. Scripps, and Cablevision (Steiner 2015).

The fact that these various outlets were owned by the same media companies that have, for decades, produced various cultural products that typically portrayed Black people in stereotypic ways means that even while there was some movement with regard to representation in the decades since *The Beulah Show*, the investment in these products still relied on audiences and audience shares. While BET (Black Entertainment Television) was for a time an independent network, it now exists as part of Viacom's holdings. And while broadcasting a program like *A Different World* marked a significant transformation in the representation of Black lives in the United States, such programs were and remain few and far between. And Black lives were still primarily relegated to the world of the situation comedy.

In 2013 Netflix began streaming serial programming; they joined the subscription cable services HBO and Showtime, and cable channels like F/X, TNT, and AMC, all of which had developed their own serial programming. Among the series in this first year of Netflix streaming was *Orange Is the New Black* (2013–19), which quickly became popular and has led to awards for several of its actors (Laverne Cox and Uzo Aduba in particular). The acting talent on *Orange* is strong, and the show provided multiple opportunities for Black women and other women of color in front of the camera even though its production team has not always included women of color in those key roles (writing, directing, producing). While possibilities for scripted drama on the "major" networks (ABC, CBS, NBC, and Fox) declined after the 2007/2008 screenwriters' strike, these other networks opened up possibilities for new scripted drama and more options for actors. Audiences flocked to the latest series, binge-watching material that in many cases reflected a diversity rarely seen in network television. Amazon and Hulu also began offering original streaming series in 2013, and YouTube Red, a pay option on YouTube that also offers original content, launched in 2018. In 2019 and early 2020, the networks decided to jump into the streaming game; CBS created CBS All Access, where it ran several programs as streaming-only (including the series Star Trek: Discovery, which featured a Black woman lead character); Disney+, which has an extended catalog of films and television programs; and Peacock, which is a streaming service of NBC programming. Finally, Apple's AppleTV+ has also gotten into content-production, launching several original series.

Aside from an occasional program that featured characters of color, however, this increasing diversity on streaming programs initially did not mark a wholesale change in the degree to which characters of color populated television scripted programming; the programming there remains largely white. Sci-fi series *Sense8* joins *Orange* as a streaming program that featured a multiracial cast and worked to avoid the stereotypes, positive and negative. But even more than the direct opportunities on cable and subscription networks, the expansion of distributive possibilities has shifted the ways people watch television and even the way that the major networks broadcast television.

The final piece of this new televisual world is the way that these changes and advances have altered how we watch television. We are now removed from the primetime season that begins in September and continues, with a brief break during late December, through April or May, with a summer season of rerun programs. Instead, networks feel comfortable contracting and purchasing limited series that may run only six to eight weeks and perhaps pick up additional seasons if those are successful. Cable networks are also not beholden to the traditional formula, and may split a show's season or broadcast two "seasons" in a single year. Streaming services may make an episode of a series available weekly or may release the entire season at once, and audiences may watch it all at the time of the release, or in smaller bites. Viewers can and do record network and cable shows by the season; networks and cable and satellite providers offer on-demand programming. So whether a show is distributed by a streaming service, a pay network, or a cable network, viewers can choose to access and binge-watch their favorite shows in a weekend or a week. These options make it possible for networks to take some risks, and for some networks, those risks have paid off.

Since the 1990s, scripted ensemble programming (which is often police procedural, law office, or hospital drama) has often been a place where some of television's diversity has remained, even after the explicitly Black programming of the 1990s waned. The attractiveness for broad audiences is that these programs often reflect their world, a kind of comfortable multiracial universe in which race exists and is sometimes explicitly engaged, sometimes not. These programs typically do not engage the "home" lives of the characters (except to occasionally create a compelling, award-seeking story line) because they are focused on the workplace. They do not engage race specifically in the ways that some of the programs we examined in previous chapters did. These are the types of programs that Kristin Warner refers to as "plastic representation"; they give numbers (especially when the industry and its critics focus on numbers) rather than "pursuing and embodying the cultural specificity of characters of color" (Warner 2017, 37). This type of programming also was generally confined to the hour-long drama, rather than the half-hour sitcom, and if we look at sitcom programming over the past decade, it was not until very recently that there have been sitcom programs that even included, let alone featured, Black actors at all. While we will not examine it in detail here because we are focused on Black women showrunners, ABC's *black-ish*, which features Tracee Ellis Ross and is a Black family comedy in the vein of *The Cosby Show*, is a notable exception on network television. I will note that Shonda Rhimes's programs exist as another kind of exception, one in which race sometimes matters but is often unstated or understated; again, we will examine these more in depth below.

For Black women in the industry, this multiply shifting landscape will open up possibilities that would not have been possible a decade earlier. I am interested in how those possibilities show up and how Black women creators navigate and negotiate this changing landscape. Has the mentoring of Black talent that allowed for the creation of *A Different World* and *Living Single* in the 1990s continued into the twenty-first century? In light of the shifting landscape, do we see more programming, and more opportunity, for Black women? And, do Black women still need to have significant credibility to get their work produced and broadcast? In what follows, we will consider four exemplars of Black women creators in the first two decades of the twenty-first century: Shonda Rhimes, who is probably the most successful Black woman television producer who established a kind of dynasty on ABC, and whose new work is on Netflix; Mara Brock Akil, who has worked with UPN and the CW; Issa Rae, who began with a web series and has worked with HBO; and Ava DuVernay, who established herself first as a film director and moved into television production—on a network owned by Oprah Winfrey. As we will see, the industry is still complicated, and creating rich depictions of Black life remains a complicated affair.

Creating Shondaland in the New Media Landscape

Shonda Rhimes's emergence as a force in network television began with her work as a writer on a number of different films, including HBO's *Introducing Dorothy Dandridge*, which starred Halle Berry, in 1999. An MFA graduate of USC's film school, Rhimes has largely considered herself a writer, even if she is most famous, now, for her creation and executive production credits. Her first attempt at a television show was a miss; she developed a pilot about war correspondents, but in 2003, with the Iraq War starting, ABC decided not to pick up the show. Still, this initial connection with ABC would bear fruit in fairly short order; Suzanne Patmore-Gibbs, an executive VP of scripted dramas at ABC, had known of Rhimes since Rhimes won a writing fellowship shortly after graduating with her MFA. Patmore-Gibbs saw the ending of NBC's scripted drama domination (*The West Wing* concluded in 2006, and *ER,* which began in 1999, had lost much of its original cast and would begin to slip in the rankings beginning in 2005), and "was championing the idea of a sexy medical drama in the post-*ER* landscape. 'We'd just bought the spec for *Desperate Housewives* and were greenlighting *Lost*,' says Patmore-Gibbs. 'NBC's golden era of *West Wing* and *ER* was ending. We needed a great ensemble drama to fill that void'" (Hunt 2011).

Thus was born *Grey's Anatomy*, perhaps Rhimes's signature show. What began as a mid-season replacement has gone on to become ABC's longest-running primetime scripted drama, and with its renewal through the spring of 2022, will become the longest running primetime medical drama on television (Ausiello 2019). As *Grey's* became a runaway hit, Rhimes would go on to executive-produce more dramas for ABC: first *Private Practice*, a spin-off of *Grey's;* then *Off the Map* (which did not take off); *Scandal*, which would be notable for starring Kerry Washington; *How to Get Away with Murder*, starring Viola Davis (which will be considered in depth in the concluding chapter); *The Catch*, which ran for two years; *For the People*, a legal drama; and *Station 19*, another spin-off from *Grey's* that charts the trials and tribulations of a group of firefighters, one of whom is married to Dr. Miranda Bailey on *Grey's* and returns for 2021–2.

Station 19 will be the last series of Rhimes's to appear on network television. She entered into a deal with Netflix, which will produce new work written and/or produced by Rhimes. In 2020, *Bridgerton* appeared, and in 2021, *Inventing Anna* appeared. As reported in *The New York Times*, Rhimes stated that

> Shondaland's move to Netflix is the result of a shared plan Ted Sarandos and I built based on my vision for myself as a storyteller and for the evolution of my company. Ted provides a clear, fearless space for creators at Netflix. He understood what I was looking for—the opportunity to build a vibrant new storytelling home for writers with the unique creative freedom and instantaneous global reach provided by Netflix's singular sense of innovation. The future of Shondaland at Netflix has limitless possibilities.
>
> (Koblin 2017)

With Rhimes as the showrunner, several of these programs have contributed to a different sensibility on television, one in which Black women can be successful in multiple ways. Rhimes's aesthetic has long been one of "color-blind casting"; characters have not been written necessarily with a particular racial or ethnic background in mind. And while some of those things are written into the script, Rhimes does not write the kinds of shows—ensemble or not—that we might consider "Black-themed." From interviews and observations of her work, it is clear that Rhimes is interested in representing a multicultural United States that for the most part is not overburdened (or overdetermined) as a place where racism is a regular feature of her characters' lives (Warner 2015). In spite of this, both *Scandal* and *How to Get Away with Murder* claim(ed) a large audience of Black *women*, who tuned in to watch these shows with Black women lead characters. I will deal with *How to Get Away with Murder* in the next chapter and will consider *Scandal* below.

In April of 2012, after the success of both *Grey's Anatomy* and *Private Practice*, Shonda Rhimes's *Scandal* hit the network. Loosely based (initially) on the life of real-life "fixer" Judy Smith, *Scandal* brought the character Olivia Pope, played by Kerry Washington, into the households of millions of viewers. And while Rhimes's programs—from her first foray with *Grey's Anatomy* to *How to Get Away with Murder (HTGAWM)*—are largely ensemble programs, they are significant in their placement of Black women in the lead or key roles in the programs.

Olivia Pope wields power in Washington DC; she began the program as the former White House press secretary who has just started her own firm for "fixing" the problems of powerful people. She and the (white, republican) president have a steamy, on-again, off-again affair that begins while she is working on his campaign. And while there's plenty about the show that's available to critique, to have a Black woman as the protagonist (arguably) of a major, successful network television show was thrilling to many Black women.[2] Certainly, we'd had the character of Bailey on *Grey's*, the attending surgeon and supervisor of the hospital's residents, among whom was the eponymous Meredith Grey. But as much as Bailey remains an important and significant character (as a surgeon, certainly), Miranda Bailey was quickly outshone by Olivia Pope. While *Grey's* is an ensemble-type program, it clearly has a protagonist (or at least a perspective), and that is Meredith Grey. And while we may have loved Bailey, her story was always still peripheral to that of Grey.

There are ways in which Olivia recalls for us the character of Julia; in her sometimes-understated elegance, in the ease in which she navigates a very white world, for example. There are other ways in which Kerry Washington, as an actor, reminds us of Diahann Carroll, not necessarily in her role as Julia, but in her role on *Dynasty*, which in terms of genre and its ensemble cast is perhaps closer to the role of Olivia. That Diahann Carroll would return to television in a recurring role on *Grey's Anatomy* is a fitting end to her career before her death in October of 2019.

There are, of course, significant differences between *Scandal* and *Julia*. Olivia arguably holds significant influence, if not power, in Washington DC, where she sometimes is hired to "fix" things for senators (or presidents) accused of infidelities or sexual harassment of young women. In fact, one of Olivia's jobs in the first season is to first deflect focus from herself to Amanda, an intern who is alleged to be having an affair with the president, before she ends up defending Amanda. Olivia's job keeps her walking the halls of power and often doing things that maintain the power structure and the status quo. As *Scandal* progressed, plots involving spies, murder, assassins, and assorted other crises would create an environment far removed from the staid, middle-class, quotidian *Julia*.

Occasionally, she represents the "little guy" against the dominant. And while some have argued that she seems "postracial," as though race has little to do with what she does or is able to accomplish, that isn't entirely true. There have been a few notable occasions on which Olivia has discussed—or at least mentioned—her race and the sometimes-uncomfortable situation of her affair with Fitzgerald Grant, the Republican president. During the second season, the president is up for reelection, and the relationship between Fitz and Olivia threatens his reelection in part because of the idea that the white president is having an affair with a Black woman. And occasionally, Shonda Rhimes creates a strongly feminist statement within the show. In s3:e6, Lisa Kudrow gets to be the mouthpiece, but Olivia has encouraged this statement against the sexism. In what is essentially a monologue, *Scandal's* writers critique both the media and the political system for its reliance on stereotype and ultimately for the way it shores up a system of (white) male supremacy:

> It's not about "experience," James. It's about gender. Reston's saying I don't have the balls to be president and he means that literally. It's offensive. It's offensive to me and to all the women whose votes he's asking for. […] And it's not just Governor Reston speaking in code about gender. It's everyone, yourself included.

Kudrow's character Josie Marcus chastises James, the reporter, for creating a "set" in her home that she demonstrates is extremely gendered:

The only reason we're doing this interview in my house is because *you* requested it. This was *your* idea and yet here you are thanking *me* for inviting you into my "lovely home." That's what you say to the neighbor lady who baked you chocolate chip cookies. This pitcher of iced tea isn't even mine. It's what your producer set here. Why? Same reason you called me a "real-life Cinderella story." It reminds people that I'm a woman without using the word. For you it's an angle, I get that. And I'm sure you think it's innocuous. But guess what, it's not.

Behind the camera, Olivia stands with Abby, at first somewhat hesitant, since Josie has appeared to go off script. But Olivia stops anyone from interrupting the interview, as Josie continues:

Don't interrupt me when I'm speaking. You're promoting stereotypes, James. You're advancing this idea that women are weaker than men. You're playing right into the hands of Reston and into the hands of every other imbecile who thinks a woman isn't fit to be Commander in Chief. Yes governor, I'm talking about you. Seven years, I served in the United States Army, which is seven more years than Governor Reston ever served.

It's these moments, in between the outrageous story lines about spies and corruption, that kept many viewers engaged, live-tweeting and watching this show in spite of the ways in which it never questions the (mostly) men in power and the corrupt ways in which they wield it. At the same time, we might note that for most of the series, Olivia's role as a "fixer" made her an ally and supporter to a white supremacist status quo, her father's command of the secret B613 and a Motown soundtrack notwithstanding.

But what exactly does Olivia give to Black women? She usually chooses what she wants for herself. She owns her sexuality—she is human, she has her weak points, and Rhimes works to make her as three-dimensional a character as possible in this often-absurd television drama. She has style. She also has a domineering father (played by Joe Morton, he runs a supersecret spy organization while a paleontologist by day) and a mother whom audiences all thought had died years before in a plane crash but was actually a spy/international criminal herself (expertly played by Khandi Alexander). Some of the plot lines are absurd, and not surprisingly so; after all, this is a nighttime drama, and absurdity is often its fodder. And while Rhimes has delivered her share of unbelievable plots and unrealistic emotionality, she is also in a position to deliver, occasionally, the ideal. In s4:e14 the story line was a "ripped from the headlines" plot where Olivia first is called in to "handle" the press and image of the DC police, one of whom has shot a young Black man, who is lying dead in the street. Olivia and her gladiators switch sides, as Olivia sympathizes with the young man's father (played adeptly by Courtney B. Vance), uncovers the white police officer's lie and racism, and gets the young man's father an audience with the president, who has also recently lost a son. And the music—Marvin Gaye and Nina Simone. Rhimes tweeted about it:

> We had a great deal of debate about this ending. Whether to be hopeful or not. It was really hard. In the end, we went with showing what fulfilling the dream SHOULD mean. The idea of possibility. And not the despair we feel now. And the despair we feel now. Ugh.
>
> (March 5, 2015)

and:

> The last image does me in. Because he's just somebody's baby. That's all. He's someone's child. #BlackLivesMatter #Scandal

And another line from that episode that reveals Rhimes behind her central character: Olivia says, "You talk about fairness and justice like it's available to everybody. It's not." But Rhimes's choice to go with the "should" rather than the reality typifies her approach to television dramas, and recalls her choice to appeal to a broad audience.

Midway through the fourth season, after Olivia has bounced from imagining a life with Fitz to playing out a fantasy life on an island with Jake, she finally puts herself first. Not ironically, immediately after the scene, when she imagines all kinds of possibilities for herself, she is kidnapped and held for ransom. Olivia believes herself to be one of the "good guys"; she is often costumed in white. By the end, audiences grew weary of the increasing absurdity of the show, which seemed to run out of steam after two terms of a Fitzgerald Grant presidency, and Rhimes chose to end the show after the seventh season. In the end, Olivia's popularity had not significantly flagged, and the show's Twitter—years after the show ended—still has 1.34 million followers. Fans engaged through the Twitter platform, live-tweeting and otherwise interacting with the actors, Rhimes, and other fans. While they sometimes bemoan Olivia's obsession with Fitz and the crazy B613 plotlines, they also revel in her successes. She is often put together, sometimes not, but mostly, she is (or had been) unique for this generation on television.

What is missing from these shows of Rhimes (it is less true of *Station 19* and *Grey's Anatomy*) is an element of *verisimilitude*. Robin Means Coleman argues that one of the reasons that Black representation has so long been relegated to the situation comedy was that sitcoms do not have to have verisimilitude (Coleman 1998, 1–2). Similarly, I argue that we can have an Olivia Pope and an Annalise Keating during the wild plots of "TGIT" (Thank God It's Thursday), because like the situation comedy, these programs lack verisimilitude as a matter of course. While Davis has created very real moments in *Murder*, the overall program overshadows those indelible moments. Black women audiences remain drawn to these programs (*Scandal* concluded after its seventh season, *Murder* after its sixth), looking for these moments of quotidian Black women's lives (like Annalise's visit to the beauty parlor during season 2, for example, or her mother's slow decline with dementia) that are altogether too few and far between.

Rhimes has also been criticized for her lack of supporting and mentoring other Black talent within the business. This aligns with Rhimes's color-blind philosophy and her creating programs in which race is not supposed to matter; however much Rhimes believes in a "postracial" world, the *facts* of the very racial (and white supremacist) nature of US society seep through her programs in ways that belie a postracial America. And while so many of the other Black women in positions of power in this study have consciously mentored young Black writing, directing, and production talent, it is not a priority for Rhimes. As we will see below, this affected Issa Rae's move to television, but more importantly, it reflects a politics that is happy to put complex Black characters on television but within a decidedly "multicultural" landscape. Rhimes's first program to be released through her Netflix deal was *Bridgerton*, a Regency-era drama that is an adaptation of Julia Quinn's novels. True to Rhimes's form, several characters are played by Black actors. The show does occasionally touch on issues of race (and it does manage to come off as not anachronistic).

Making It Work: Mara Brock Akil

Mara Brock Akil began her television career working as a writer and producer on the UPN sitcom *Moesha* in the late 1990s. She would go on to create several series—*Girlfriends*, which debuted in 2000 and ran for eight seasons; *The Game*, which was a spin-off of *Girlfriends* and ran for three seasons on the CW and for an additional six seasons on BET; *Being Mary Jane*, which ran on BET for four seasons (and recently concluded with a two-hour episode); *Black Lightning*, a Black superhero series that currently airs on the CW; and *Love Is…*, cocreated with her husband Salim Akil for OWN (Oprah Winfrey Network). Brock Akil has become successful at negotiating the television production landscape; she has continued to develop Black-themed shows *specifically*, and her programs have taken up Black life and Black experience. That her shows have consistently been broadcast on networks known for narrowcasting (CW, BET, and OWN) also reveals the extent to which, in this new media landscape, Blackness on television is still considered a niche market. While *Girlfriends* was the start of Brock Akil's career as a showrunner and creator, it is clear that her career was significantly enhanced by the development of new technologies that allowed for success outside of the major networks. She relates:

> Technology has changed our industry, and I think that's opened up different revenue streams and ways to make money and distribute television. It's made the global conversation easier, quicker. The analytics of just social media has also sustained my career. My audience was able to show themselves.
>
> (Kameir 2016)

Her experience working on both *Moesha* and *The Jamie Foxx Show* made her a reasonable risk for UPN, which had already been heavily invested in creating programming for a Black audience since its debut in the 1990s. Brock Akil was a known quantity, and the format of her program—four Black women friends and their interactions—had already been shown to be highly successful with Bowser's *Living Single* in the 1990s. In spite of this, UPN was not completely on board. As she related in an interview with *The Fader* in 2016:

> *Girlfriends*, for instance—nobody would touch it. I went straight to UPN and sold it. So I go to the studios, like, "Hello guys, I have a show—who wants it?" Nobody wanted it. No studio wanted to be the financier of that, even though it was already sold. That's how Kelsey Grammer got involved. He still had money left on his development slate at Paramount/Viacom. I appreciate him having the business acumen to be like, "Oh shit, she sold it, let's roll! There's no work to do."
>
> (Kameir 2016)

Girlfriends extends the successful formula of the Black-woman-centered sitcom and acts as a kind of bridge between the groundbreaking programming of the 1990s with the new developments in the 2010s.

Girlfriends itself draws on the familiar tropes of the Black-woman-friends program of which *Living Single* was a primary example. Both *Living Single* and *Girlfriends* bookend the popular HBO program about four white woman friends, *Sex and the City*. And while the character types between the programs are similar, and we might see *Girlfriends* as a Black *Sex and the City*, its characters are specifically *Black* character types. In other ways, however, the comparison might not be unrealistic. Tracee Ellis Ross plays Joan, a lawyer who has just made junior partner in her firm, and the other core characters are three of her friends—Toni, the materialistic friend; Maya, the working-class assistant who works for Joan but becomes a friend; and Lynn, the political college student. The women are joined by Joan's male work colleague, William, whose role in the show grows after the first season. *Girlfriends* shares the inclusion of men among the core characters with *Living Single*, a departure from *Sex and the City*, in which the core characters are only the women. We can see this inclusion as a marker of a Black feminist aesthetic, in which *women* are not so separate from men and where writers are thinking about an inclusive Black community even while focusing on the lives and experiences of Black women. Maya is married, but all of the other characters are single. Joan is the marriage-seeker and the one who most embodies the "Black lady" trope. The show takes place in Los Angeles, but its locations are not very specific (we know it is LA because of shots of street signs of familiar Los Angeles area streets and shots of downtown LA). And while Maya is working class, and Toni has working-class roots, the show is comfortably situated in a Black middle-class world.

Like its predecessors in the 1990s, *Girlfriends* manages to entertain with lots of plots centered around romance and marriage even as it occasionally deals with serious issues. Its run length—eight seasons, making it the longest-running Black-themed sitcom—means that the show occasionally dealt with serious issues even though, for the most part, its plots were slightly different articulations of the same issues around romance.[3] The choice to include William as a core character among the "Girlfriends" is an interesting one. On the one hand, he provides an intriguing kind of male presence, one that is at once both engaged with a kind of hegemonic Black masculinity—one that is educated, professional, and middle class—while on the other hand, he is also both somewhat nerdy and "conservative" (he does refer to himself as conservative in one episode). As mentioned earlier, this inclusion also reveals a Black feminist aesthetic that includes men and various masculinities in representations of Blackness. William's trials and tribulations are also engaged during the series (especially his romantic involvements). There is a subtle undercurrent of potential partnership between Joan and William for much of the early seasons, and it is a familiar trope to keep a subtle sense of both attraction and unrequited love (on the part of William, for the most part) as something that moves the series along.

While there are similarities between *Girlfriends* and *Living Single*, the feel and aesthetic of the show are quite different. Where *Living Single* embraced and retained a hip-hop feel, *Girlfriends* shifts away from that aesthetic. It embraces different kinds of Black womanhood, although they are "types" that we might have associated with McMillan's work in the 1990s (something *Living Single* was supposed to have done, but didn't). In part, this is because of the ages of the friends of the title (who are older and somewhat more mature than the friends of *Living Single*). *Girlfriends* is less youthful than *Living Single*, with the slightly more serious issues and concerns of Black women about a decade older. This is an age of marriage and children (none of the women on *Living Single* were at the point of having children, even if they were concerned with the issue of marriage) and advancing in work situations and opportunities. The mixture of class positions—the junior partner and the working-class administrative assistant, for example—provides Brock Akil a way to talk more broadly about the diversity of Black experience in the United States.

In season 6, Brock Akil created a spin-off of *Girlfriends*, focused on Joan's niece who gives up a spot at a top medical school in order to be with her boyfriend, who has just been signed to a professional football team. *The Game*, which ran from 2006 to 2015 (and had a two-hour concluding episode in 2019), focused on the women who were wives and girlfriends of professional football players. While I will not discuss episodes of the show here, that Brock Akil would create and produce another long-running series for the CW is testament to their commitment to her as an artist. But no program is secure, even for a veteran like Brock Akil. After three seasons on the CW, *The Game* was cancelled; its following was significant enough that BET picked up the program for an additional six seasons after moving the production location to Atlanta.

Brock Akil's primary series during the 2010s was *Being Mary Jane,* which ran on BET and had a significant following. Her most recent series, *Black Lightning* for the CW, while part of the CW's DC superhero series (*Arrow, Supergirl,* etc.), could almost be considered a Black family drama, as it examines the lives of the Black family and its interactions within a Black community in the era of Black Lives Matter (with a dad and two daughters who have superpowers, and a mom who's a scientist).

Black Lightning is a cooperative venture between Brock Akil and husband Salim Akil (Akil is documented as "showrunner," although both are executive producers). *Black Lightning* concluded its run in spring of 2021. The show puts Black families and communities at its core; when the series begins, Jefferson

Pierce/Black Lightning is a high school principal in Freeland, which is a predominantly Black city, and features Black heroes and villains. The program quickly takes up issues of organized crime, drug addiction, and medical experimentation on communities of color. Its references to contemporary situations of violence in and against communities of color make it timely, even while it also harnesses the rising interest of multiple audiences in Afrofuturism and the Black Fantastic (including comics and superheroes). The show also features the first Black lesbian superhero on television, one of Black Lightning's two daughters (both of whom have superpowers). Like other programs that Brock Akil has produced, it is unashamedly a "Black" show and features issues of concern to Black communities. The women of *Black Lightning* include not only the superpowered daughters Thunder and Lightning but scientists, villains, victims, and heroes. In short, the program develops a "whole" Black community in which there are multiple ways of being Black. In 2020, Brock Akil signed a deal with Netflix, where new programming is likely to come (Andreeva).

Brock Akil's career shows not only how it is possible for Black women to have success in the industry but also its challenges and pitfalls. Without the assistance of Kelsey Grammer, *Girlfriends* would not have been made, even after UPN bought the idea. Brock Akil's continued success has been rooted in networks that market to audiences interested in Black stories. Certainly, Black women showrunners can have success working with networks whose core audiences are Black (BET, OWN) or who have interest in narrowcasting to Black markets.

Issa Rae Is (Not) Awkward and Insecure

With the advent of YouTube in 2005, a platform for sharing and streaming video emerged. YouTube made it possible to share and stream video across multiple devices, initially on desktop and laptop computers. Video editing software increased amateur videographers' ability to generate and post content, and for consumers of that content to find it. And in 2011, an aspiring writer-director-actor known as Issa Rae slipped into the developing streaming-video scene with a series she titled *The Misadventures of Awkward Black Girl*.

The Misadventures of Awkward Black Girl (*ABG*) was Rae's third attempt at developing programming on the web. Produced by Rae and directed by Shea William Vanderpoort, *ABG* recounts the life of "J," an "awkward" Black twenty-something as she deals with work, life, and romance. Not only was the program distributed on social media but social media was where the show "lived," in a way; it was talked about on Facebook and Twitter, from which its popularity grew. Rae's YouTube channel has over 350,000 subscribers, and *ABG* won a Shorty award in 2012 (Rae 2016). *ABG* is popular in part because it is irreverent, at least in the sense that it feels no responsibility to present some imagined, two-dimensional Black womanhood. "J" is not like the "positive" middle-class "ladies" from the 1980s and owes something to the young Black women, in their variety, who were featured on *Living Single* and *A Different World* (Villareal 2015). She is an "awkward" twenty-something who works at a job she hates with a variety of people who are often also awkward and weird. J writes "ratchet" rap lyrics to work out her issues around work and romance.

ABG's popularity is testament to its appeal across age, gender, and racial groups. J's world is multiracial, and J as a character reveals some of the complexities of Black life in the current age. Issa Rae is not alone; user-created content that highlights the diversity of Black life, explicitly including Black queer and trans life, has emerged and is beginning to thrive on social media. In fact, the combination of content that is specifically "entertainment" and that offers critical perspectives on popular culture (e.g., Franchesca Ramsey's work) helps to nurture an audience ready for different content.[4] In spite of the fact that J's world is multiracial, the show is not trying to represent a postracial world. If anything, it reveals the contours of a world that believes itself to be postracial while being decidedly racialized. As Jenna Wortham says, the show is "seamless blend of race politics and Seinfeldian situational comedy" (2015).

ABG began with very short pieces; episode 1 is less than five minutes long. J befriends one person at work, Cici, and the two of them (realizing they are both awkward) become fast friends. J manages her terrible call-center job, dodging the immediate supervisor, a Black woman who is obnoxious and with whom she has conflict, and the company's white owner. At the end of the first season, J begins a relationship with a white man, Jay, providing Rae with an abundance of material about J's conflicted feelings about interracial dating. As the series goes on, the episodes are longer and more involved.

The surprising popularity of *ABG* did attract attention from people in the industry. Unfortunately, it was not the kind of attention that Rae really wanted. As Wortham notes, those production companies that expressed an interest in *ABG* wanted to make it something completely different—witness the "network executive who wanted to make it into a pan-racial franchise operation, starting with 'Awkward Indian Boy.' Another suggested Rae recast the lead with a lighter-skinned actress with long, straight hair—in essence, the exact opposite of Rae. She turned down the offers" (Wortham 2015). For someone who grew up on 1990s Black-themed television, Rae looked to those programs—including specifically *A Different World* and *Living Single*—as the model of what she was interested in creating. Rae even met with Rhimes and Betsy Beers, who considered her show idea of "I Hate L.A. Dudes." There was initial interest, but Rae struggled with the feedback from the network and from Rhimes's team. Acknowledging the importance of this opportunity, Rae commented that "that was my very first experience, and to be under Shonda and Betsy [Beers] was the ultimate learning experience because, hello, they're killing it. I learned about the studio and network system, how much money goes into making shows, how long it takes, how much ownership is important" (Villareal 2015). Rae's vision of the kind of work she wanted to do was too important to abandon, and she wasn't willing to make the kind of show that Rhimes and Beers wanted. Rae said, "I compromised my vision, and it didn't end up the show that I wanted," she says. "'It wasn't funny anymore'" (Wortham 2015).

Fortunately for Rae, there was interest that would lead to something. A year after the initial work with Rhimes, Rae was contacted by an executive at HBO. She had another idea for a show; much like the series that got her started, the idea for *Insecure* was at least semi-autobiographical and would center on a Black woman nearing thirty who was dealing with personal and professional challenges. It's a story that finds resonances not only in the coveted 18–24 age demographic but in others who have also been through that awkward age. This time, it would be Larry Wilmore (mostly of Comedy Central fame, but who had worked extensively in Black-themed television before that work) who would provide the mentoring and the production assistance. HBO said yes to the show, but Rae struggled to get the production staff that she wanted. "Rae was excited to hire a support staff of other nonwhite directors and producers who would be intimately familiar with the milieu inhabited by her characters. She had a wish list of people she liked—primarily young women of color—but she soon found out HBO had little interest in hiring them" (Wortham 2015). The network did give her Prentis Penny; Penny was a veteran Black showrunner who had gotten his start in television with Brock Akil on *Girlfriends*. That connection, and Penny's experience, enabled Rae's vision to be realized.

Insecure's first season debuted in the summer of 2016 on HBO. It was clear that *ABG* was a foundational text for the show, as some of the elements of *ABG* (most notably the dysfunctional workplace) made the transition to *Insecure*. Both shows are also set in Los Angeles; unlike the Los Angeles of *Girlfriends,* with its middle-class sensibilities and Westside neighborhoods, Rae sets her programs in South Central. To locate the shows in an area of Los Angeles that is not only coded specifically as "Black" but also was historically the site of Black rebellion (from the Watts rebellion to the Rodney King riots, as well as having been the site of numerous Black films from the 1990s, Rae's formative years) makes a statement both about Black life in the 2010s and about Black community. I see this as one of Rae's key interventions in the refiguring of Black representation; her choice of South Central, and her representations of Black people of different socioeconomic classes within the show, shifts "South Central" and indeed *Blackness* in the consciousness of the viewing public. Ultimately, Rae's artistic choices in scripting, casting, and in the mise-en-scene of program continue the work in which Black women producers and writers have been engaged for two decades: challenging traditional narratives about African American lives. The opening up of representations outside of the narrow confines of stereotyped Blackness, and the proliferation of these additional images, can work to resignify or reframe mythologies of Black life in the United States.

While clearly Rae has been and continues to be influenced by the work of showrunners Allen, Bowser, and Brock Akil, her sensibilities are her own. The YouTube platform on which Rae initially broadcast *ABG* allowed her to develop an aesthetic style that appeals strongly to audiences in their twenties. *Insecure's* twenty-something viewers (and some older than their twenties) immediately identify with the character Issa's trials and tribulations, the hip-hop soundtrack, and the world that *Insecure* portrays. Initially, she lives with her boyfriend Lawrence, who has been without a job for a while, and whom Issa sees as not really trying to get out and support himself. They are at a point in their relationship when Issa feels uninspired and bored; lots of other men start to look good. Lawrence, on the other hand, sees himself as destined for a good job and isn't really interested in taking a job until he can land the "good" one, but he ultimately does start working at a Best Buy-type store near the end of season 1 in order to try to keep Issa happy. Lawrence's character deals with structural racism as a Black man, and we see that through his frustrations with underemployment.

Issa's best friend Molly is a successful lawyer. We might see her as a direct contrast to Joan from *Girlfriends*; Molly is also the only Black woman lawyer in her firm. Molly also has relationship issues; she wants to be in a relationship with an "equal" and avoids men who are less educated and whom she deems less "successful." Neither Issa nor Molly is particularly good at relationships.

Molly is mostly successful at work, even while Issa relates her frustration at her job, which creates programming for "inner city youth." Both Issa and Molly are tokens in their workplaces, a point which Rae makes clear frequently puts them in awkward positions vis-à-vis their colleagues and superiors. For Issa, this means she is the one person who works at her job who "understands" the Black and brown kids in the youth program—which, from the first episode, we see is a mistaken assumption. Issa may be Black, but she is also clearly middle-class and has difficulty relating to the kids, who quickly call her out. As the show moves into season 2, there is less a focus on work and more a focus on relationships. Issa and Lawrence have broken up, and Issa is theoretically enjoying her freshly single status. In season 2, Issa tries to work out what she wants in a boyfriend, and Lawrence, while his new-found success should make him happy, he still thinks about Issa (in episode 4, after being picked up in the grocery store by two young white women who take him home for sex, finds himself parked outside of the Issa's building). The third season will deal more strongly with issues of masculinity; while these issues were present in seasons 1 and 2, they are more sharply in focus in the third season. In the fourth season, Rae considers friendships between women, as Molly and Issa's relationship is challenged. To work through issues around Black masculinities, especially as they are encountered by Black women, is one of the things that mark this as an important, and intersectional, comedy.

The directing and photography in *Insecure* render Issa's Los Angeles, in all its variety (from South Central to Westwood), "normal" space. There isn't a differentiation between the care given to Molly's expensive apartment or Issa's more moderately priced one. Rae resignifies South Central not as a place relegated to violence and poverty but as a livable space occupied by "regular" people. Most importantly, Rae shows Los Angeles's Black population as diverse in socioeconomic class, education, skin color—a broader picture of Blackness than is typically available in most television, and particularly in the situation comedy. These representations also include a variety of Black masculinities, another significant departure. In Issa's fully realized world, we see young Black people living whole lives. There is no pressure to be the perfect "Black ladies" of the 1980s or even the generally "respectable" representations of *Different World*, *Living Single*, and even *Girlfriends*. *Insecure* concluded in fall of 2021 after its fifth season. Rae has gone on to produce *A Black Lady Sketch Show*, *Sweet Life Los Angeles*, and has four additional projects she is currently executive producing.

From *Selma* to New Orleans:
Ava DuVernay Touches Television

Director Ava DuVernay, who emerged into the spotlight with her award-winning film *Selma* in 2014, also entered the television world (although on OWN, the Oprah Winfrey Network) with an hour-long drama that centers on three generations of a Black family in Louisiana. *Queen Sugar* premiered in the summer of 2016 and focuses on the lives of the Bordelon children after the death of their father, a sugar cane farmer.

DuVernay began as a publicist, working in both film and television, starting in 1999. She moved into directing and producing in the mid-2000s, beginning with her first short film, *Saturday Night Life*. Most of DuVernay's work prior to *Selma* was documentary filmmaking; her first documentary, *This Is the Life* (2008) was the first of several documentaries she would direct and/or produce that focused on music.

In 2016, after DuVernay's success with *Selma* and simultaneous with the release of her documentary *13*, *Queen Sugar* premiered. *Queen Sugar* emerged as something unique in that moment on television—an hour-long drama about a Black family. This is significant, because it marks a shift in the industry, one in which Black people, as stars in their own shows, can engage in this genre within the medium where it has never been welcome before. It follows the short-lived James Earl Jones vehicle *Under One Roof* in late 1995 and the Showtime production *Soul Food*, based on George Tillman Jr.'s film of the same name. Its location on OWN and availability on Amazon Prime video make it available to a large audience, and its support from Oprah gives it a kind of credibility with Black audiences. *Queen Sugar* stands outside of other hour-long and even half-hour-long programming on OWN, notably the various offerings from Tyler Perry and reality-based programming.

Queen Sugar follows the experiences of the Bordelon children—Charly, Ralph Angel, and Nova—and their aunt Violet after the death of their father early in the first season. In addition to the core, there are also the next generation, Charly's son Micah and Ralph Angel's son Blue. The program is explicitly political in many instances. First, the sugar cane farm that the children inherit is threatened by the white landowners who once owned the Bordelon family and who dominate the sugar cane processing business in this part of Louisiana. Ralph Angel is an ex-con who initially struggles with finding employment after his release from jail. Nova, the newspaper journalist, takes up as her causes police brutality specifically and racism more broadly (which generates a conflict for her with her then-boyfriend, a married white police officer). Charly deals with her basketball-player-husband's infidelity and their divorce. Blue's mother, Darla, struggles with an opioid addiction. Certainly, there are a lot of contemporary issues infused throughout the program. What keeps the show from becoming too melodramatic is the human complexity of the characters and the skill of the acting. As Rutina Wesley said in the special hosted by Oprah at the end of season 2, the stories are "universal stories of family" (Unknown 2018). Kofe Sidibe, who plays Ralph Angel, comments in the program that Ralph Angel "could have been a stereotype"; perhaps, in taking on the various issues of the show (mass incarceration, Civil War monuments, police brutality) it might indeed have become a caricature of itself.

While it would certainly be possible to discuss in depth the various plots that have developed over the first two seasons of the show, that is perhaps somewhat less important than what the show *signifies* and does. This is a show that embraces dark skin, highlighted by lighting designers and directors of photography who are skilled at filming dark skin. In a television world where Black skin tones are medium to light, aesthetically *Queen Sugar* sets a new standard. The *look* of the show is different because of how the show is shot, and who is shooting it. The filming evokes a love for Black skin tones that is typically not present in other kinds of programming (Figure 6).

Figure 6 Bordelon family dinner from *Queen Sugar*.

The deliberate choice on the part of DuVernay and Winfrey to hire Black women directors, and to have a writing staff made up primarily of women, carries forward the tradition and ideas that existed (albeit in limited fashion) in Hattie McDaniel's imagination, and which we saw develop in part with Debbie Allen's work on *Different World*. This is the culmination of that work in a significant way; it demonstrates what kinds of things are possible when the production of media and culture is in the hands of Black women (and other Black folk) as creators. As Oprah says during the season finale special, "It feels like an imagined dream fulfilled. It's the kind of show I envisioned when I started this network. I didn't know it was possible but you [DuVernay] made it so. You all [audience] made it so" (Unknown 2018).

The ability of the show's characters and plots to resonate with Black viewers is evident by audience members' comments. To have Violet as an "older" woman who is a sexual being breaks with previous stereotypes. One audience member, whose son was a victim of police brutality, spoke poignantly about the verisimilitude of the plot about Micah and his encounter with a violent, racist police officer. The show is an opportunity to reimagine and reform representations of both Black womanhood and Black manhood in significant ways. It is an opportunity to "show families loving each other who are black people" (Unknown 2018). The revisioning of both Black family life and of Black fatherhood gives audiences another representation of Black life that has been all too rare on television.

Finally, the construction of the characters as complex, multidimensional people contributes to its verisimilitude and its radical representations of Black people. None of the Black characters are flawless (or completely flawed). There is not a sense that it is necessary to promote "positive" representations, or to focus on "respectable" middle-class Blackness.

These four Black women showrunners have had significant impact on the contemporary television world. Their access to power in the industry was hard-won, but their contributions to the medium have made it possible for us to enjoy a wider variety of Black representation on television. Finally, we will return to the stage actor, as we consider how established and younger Black women are impacting the television landscape.

Conclusion: Negotiating Hollywood

In the fall of 2016, Rhimes's television dominance continued with the premiere of *How to Get Away with Murder* on ABC. The show was produced by Rhimes and starred Viola Davis, whose long stage and film career inspired a reconsideration, to some degree, of the influence a skilled and award-winning actor can have in television programming.

We began this journey through Black women's involvement in television with a look at *The Beulah Show* and the kinds of influence that two of the actors, Ethel Waters and Hattie McDaniel, tried to exert on the program. Over the decades, skilled Black women actors crossed from the stage (and film, to a lesser degree) to the small screen. Accustomed to the collaborative process that is the theatre, where actors do script and character study to flesh out a character, Diahann Carroll and Esther Rolle took on television roles in the hopes of shifting the characters they were playing into ones they could be proud of. The actors' political commitments—they were committed to Civil Rights struggles—made them critical of the roles they took on because they were well aware of the power of representations to shape perceptions and understandings of minoritized people. When actors ran up against limits to their influence, they looked to other ways to shape representations to create different understandings of Black life in America. They emerged as directors, writers, and producers and found a modicum of success in creating different kinds of representations of Black life.

However, the day of the influential actor is not over, although that actor influence looks different today than it did in 1950. Here, I want to focus on Viola Davis, who starred in and executive produced *How to Get Away with Murder*, as both a way to look back at the history of Black women in television and to consider how actors can and do still negotiate their positions in the industry. We will also consider three other actors/creators who are currently influencing the televisual world: Regina King, Janelle Monáe, and Marsai Martin.

How to Get Away with … Pushing the Industry (Spring 2020)

Davis became interested in acting while in high school in Rhode Island. She studied theatre as an undergraduate and later graduated from Julliard, where she honed her acting skills. She worked in theatre, winning an Obie Award in 1999, and continued to take on smaller parts in film and television, as well as in the theatre, until she was cast in August Wilson's play *King Hedley II* in 2001. Her performance in *King Hedley II* earned her a Tony award, and it also opened doors for her in Hollywood. Her next award nomination would come for her supporting role in the film *Doubt* (2008). She would go on to star in a stage revival of *Fences* (2010), which would not only win her another Tony award but also set the stage for a film version, in which she costarred with Denzel Washington (2016). While her work in *Doubt* earned her an Academy Award nomination, it was her role in *The Help* (2011) that would popularize her with wider audiences. When she was cast as Annalise Keating in *How to Get Away with Murder* (*HTGAWM*), she was recognizable to broader audiences due to her success in film and theatre. Her virtuosity—certainly, the Tony award is a testament to her acting skill—also enabled her to assert some authority when it came to the character of Annalise.

On the surface, there are a number of similarities between Shonda Rhimes's dramas *Scandal* and *HTGAWM*. Obviously, like *Scandal*, we have a Black woman as the protagonist (ostensibly, for while the show is somewhat an ensemble, it clearly revolves around Annalise). Annalise Keating is a savvy defense lawyer teaching a course in defense strategies at a law school in Philadelphia. She wields power and is highly intelligent—she is known for getting her clients off (hence the title). Like *Scandal*, she is initially involved with (in this case married to) a white man (until his death).

Also like *Scandal*, *HTGAWM* begins with a murder—in this case, the murder of Lila, a young sorority member at the college where both Annalise and her husband teach. Even while Annalise takes on other cases, she is persuaded to take the case of the young, working-class woman who has been accused of the murder. Like Olivia Pope, Annalise surrounds herself with a multiracial group of workers. Her interns—a multiracial, queer-inclusive set of smart law students—help her in the primary case and with others. And Annalise as a character is captivating. Her court argumentation is brutally honest, and she enjoys being a champion of the "little guy." In subsequent years, plots focused on other murders that spiral out to involve more than the students in her immediate circle. There was even a *Scandal-HTGAWM* crossover, where Annalise argues a case before the Supreme Court on a class-action suit championing inmates (particularly Black inmates) who had ineffective counsel during their trials. There are just enough of these kinds of cases and moments to keep the progressive audience coming back, despite the absurd situations and tangled plotlines.

But the casting of Viola Davis—a dark-skinned Black woman as a protagonist—defies the logic of Hollywood beauty standards that prefer lighter skin and usually long, straight hair—certainly Kerry Washington or Halle Berry as a "type." And where Olivia Pope looks comfortable in her designer clothes, Annalise does not. In fact, it was Davis's choice for Annalise to walk awkwardly in heels. It is this depth of Davis's character development that kept me watching the program. Davis is a virtuoso, and because her training and much of her work has been on the stage, she approaches acting differently. She thinks about her character, about who her character has been and how those things (that sometimes actors make up) affect the way the character is and what the character says and does. This is why we see the character trait of Annalise being "uncomfortable in heels."[1] And this is why Davis insisted upon doing many scenes in ways that are unusual for television but that reveal character in a very theatrical way.

The first of these came during season 1, when Davis chose to portray Annalise's bedtime routine, which included removing a wig and her makeup. The camera focuses in on her as she first takes off her jewelry, then removes her straightened bob wig and false eyelashes, then forcefully removes her makeup with a cloth. She is silent as music plays over the scene. The choice to remove her wig and makeup—to reveal, in this moment, her dark, unadorned skin as well as the complicated relationship Black women have had with the pressure to straighten their hair and the consequences of that for hair damage and loss—reveals something intrinsic to Black women's lives. Her anger at her husband, whom she begins to suspect of having murdered Lila, and the concomitant sadness are so strongly and clearly evoked. Her relationship with her husband is contentious, and we learn more about him as the series progresses, just as we learn more about her. If we want a deeply flawed character, Annalise is it. We learn that her husband was once her therapist (leaving us to question his moral compass), who in fits of anger reveals things about her past that he most likely knows because of that relationship. We later discover that she also has a contentious relationship with her mother—but more on that in a moment.

The choice to cast Davis, a veteran stage and film actor with multiple awards to her name, recalls the choices in earlier decades to cast accomplished actors to draw audiences and anchor a program. There is a fundamental difference here, though; unlike in the earlier decades, when Black actors' perspectives on character were ignored, Rhimes's presence as an executive producer on *HTGAWM* may have created an environment where such recommendations were heeded rather than ignored.

Interestingly, while Rhimes is an executive producer, she is not the creator of the show—that honor falls to Peter Nowalk, who is neither Black nor female. And the show has received a variety of responses. Alessandra Stanley, a white television critic for the *New York Times*, accused Rhimes of creating a show about an "angry black woman" (to which Rhimes responded that Nowalk was the show's creator) (Stanley 2014). Commenters on Twitter and other social media platforms have bemoaned the show's abundant sex scenes—especially ones between men. Its "crazy" plots have outpaced even *Scandal* (which became more and more absurd until the end), and for this reason, some viewers tuned it out. And while it's easy to stop at the show's surface, once you dig a bit deeper, there's something interesting and profound going on. As a part of ABC's #TGIT lineup and with some 918,000 Twitter followers, it held audience attention and retained some redeeming qualities, which I will outline below.

In *HTGAWM*, Rhimes and Nowalk engage race, gender, and class in what are, for television, novel ways. Michaela, one of Annalise's interns, is a type-A, assertive, and bright young Black woman who seems to have it all, including a fiancé from a wealthy Black family. But Michaela is playing a role; and when she begins to doubt her fiancé's love for her, she breaks off the engagement, to the dismay of her would-be mother-in-law, played by Lynn Whitfield. In another classic scene from the first season, Michaela asserts herself—with echoes of Olivia Pope, but from a completely different class position. With her working-class, rural roots, Michaela stands up to the pretentious Black upper-middle-class woman, declaring in her refusal to continue her engagement that she loves herself, even if her fiancé does not. We watch Michaela as she consistently chooses as mentors (or aspires to be like) Black women from working-class backgrounds. Her drive to be successful clearly flies in the face of the stereotypes of Black working-class people.

Annalise's contentious relationship with her mother is revealed in this same episode. Davis related a story about how Annalise's mother became a character and how Cicely Tyson came to play her. Davis encouraged Nowalk to include more of Annalise's life story and thought that the inclusion of her mother would be an important element. Nowalk agreed but did not know who might play that role; Davis, who had always wanted to work with Tyson, recommended her (Davis 2016). It was thanks to Davis's influence that the following exchange was ever written and that viewers were treated to these two highly skilled actors creating a moving scene. Annalise reveals to the audience that she was sexually molested by an uncle who lived with them; she blames her mother for allowing the abuse to continue. Cicely Tyson, playing her mother, eventually relents and gives Annalise the full story. Annalise sits on the floor while her mother sits on the bed and proceeds to comb out Annalise's hair and share her secret:

> I bought that house over off Peachtree when I was pregnant with you. I was so proud of that house; wasn't much but it was mine. Built a porch swing, tended a little garden that was just right out front … I would bake up a storm on that old stove, you know, the ones that you would have to light with a long match? (chuckles) And one winter, Uncle Clyde came by and said he needed a place to stay. Just till he got on his feet, he said. Can't turn your back on your family! And then one day, I woke up in the middle of the night. I don't know what it was—I just—woke up. I walked down the hall to look in on you, and *Clyde* came out of your room and I knew what he had done.

At this moment, Annalise looks up at her mother, who continues:

> He was a big man. Like his liquor. His hooch. Smoked three packs of cigarettes a day, was always stinking up the house with cigarette smoke. [getting angry]. All the time, he would fall asleep on the couch, that cigarette hanging out of his mouth. I would go by and put it out, and one night, not too long after, he fell asleep on the couch, drunk as a skunk, that cigarette hanging out of his mouth. I got you and your brothers and sisters out of bed and went over to Aunt Mabel's to sleep. And that night, that house that I loved so much, burned to the ground. And your uncle Clyde burned right with it. Oh I know how you've been torturing yourself about what went on here baby, maybe you did something real bad, I don't know and don't much care if you did. I know if you did, you had your reasons. Sometimes, you gotta do what you gotta do. Even if all you've got is a long match and a very flammable hooch.

She finally looks down at Annalise, who returns her look, both of them understanding the sacrifice that her mother made to stop the abuse (Figure 7).

These moments are possible on television in part because Shonda Rhimes puts her name behind them, even when she does not explicitly write them. They show us types of Black womanhood that have rarely been seen on

Figure 7 Cicely Tyson and Viola Davis scene from *How to Get Away with Murder*.

television. Olivia and Annalise are women for whom we cheer, even while we wince at their flaws. That we can have Black female (lead) characters who aren't perfect, who don't do everything right, is in itself a positive change. We have left behind the days when only the perfect "Black lady" could be counted as a "positive" representation. Indeed, to view the televisual more critically means that we are often looking beyond the "positive" representation so deeply mired in respectability politics. At the same time, Rhimes's "genre"—these programs that are essentially ensemble pieces that prominently feature Black women—can only push television representation so far. While I applaud much of the exceptional work that Davis has done in creating a character in Annalise Keating that is a multidimensional person in a two-dimensional world, there is a limit to the potential influence of this character on the larger world of representation.

Davis is not one dimensional, however. For her, the core of taking on or creating a role lies in the script; writing is an essential part of getting to that three-dimensional character that has the potential to come alive when performed by a skilled actor. She says, "I'm always drawn to the writing because it starts there first. That is why people can read scripts online and know a year in advance who is going to be nominated for an Oscar based on what's on the page. Because if it's not on the page, how can you play it?" (Smye 2015). Realizing this, she and husband Julius Tennon created their own production company:

> She calls her JuVee Productions a "walking metaphor" of inclusion, noting that she has people of color and members of the LGBTQ community on staff at every level. "Women are at the forefront of just about every project," she adds.

She started JuVee Productions with her husband, Julius Tennon, in 2011 so she could have more of a voice in her own career, as well as provide more diversity on set. Before that, Davis says, she often felt left out of the conversation.

(Press 2019)

Davis and Tennon have produced a film documentary (*Emanuel*, about the murders of nine African Americans in a South Carolina church); a documentary series (*The Last Defense*, about several death row cases, designed to reveal the structural racism in the criminal justice system), and the two-season series *American Koko*, which was broadcast on ABC's streaming service and garnered an Emmy nomination for its lead actor, Diarra Kilpatrick. They have quite a few projects on the docket.

Davis added "executive producer" to her role on *HTGAWM*. Between this and her work with JuVee Productions, she has perhaps finally found the formula that Hattie McDaniel looked for so many years before: a way to exert significant influence over a television show. Davis and McDaniel, both of whom won Oscars for playing maids—roles over which they both received pushback—were able to translate that status into visibility for white audiences. But where McDaniel struggled to create better characters out of limited scripts, Davis has set her own terms, both by creating her own production company and by (finally) picking and choosing her roles. But this comes with the hard work of decades, with the experience and resources to ensure that you can create (to some extent) the work that you want to do. In an interview, Davis relates that "If you're a black actor— especially actress—who gets to any level of power and you say, 'I'm going to produce my own film and I'm going to be the lead in the film,' you need a No. 2 who's going to get that film international distribution. That means you need a big white star" (Ugwu 2018)—or at least someone that Hollywood believes will "sell" internationally.

And as I complete this project, another moment of "full circle" emerges. Viola Davis was selected to reprise Esther Rolle's Florida Evans role on a live re-creation of *Good Times*. Joined by Andre Braugher as James and Tiffany Haddish as Willona, the program recreation (produced by Norman Lear, Jimmy Kimmel, and Kerry Washington) continues a trend begun in the spring of 2019 of filming live episode remakes of *All in the Family* and *The Jeffersons*. Pondering the two actors—Rolle and Davis—side by side, considering their significant stage careers and their work specifically in Black theatre, it seems appropriate that Davis would reprise Rolle's character. The program was billed as a "holiday" episode, although there was never an explicit Christmas episode in the original series.

The episode they chose to reprise was from season 3, from November 1975, in which James and Florida argue over two different candidates for alderman for their Chicago ward. James supports the incumbent, an older Black man who has been the alderman for decades; Florida (and Willona, Thelma, and Michael) supports the young, up-and-coming challenger. This recreation also featured John Amos in an appearance as the older alderman, a casting move that was well received by the audience (even though at times, Amos seemed lost on stage or to have forgotten his lines).

Davis's Florida/Rolle was well acted, and her careful study of Rolle's mannerisms and the program provided a sense of seeing Rolle again, almost. The choice of this episode, which came before the tilt to the J. J. character, set audiences up for a chance to fondly remember the series at its height. The politics of this episode—older incumbent versus young challenger—translates well to the current state of politics, perhaps, and certainly shows the longevity and "universality" of some of Lear's work. The connections between Rolle and Davis, accomplished stage actors with profound political opinions, make that connection between them (and their places in this project) more profound.

Regina King, from Acting to Directing

The recent success of Black women in moving from acting roles to work in directing and producing is further evidenced by the developing career of Regina King. King, who began her acting career at the age of fourteen on the set of *227*, has emerged as a force in Hollywood—in both television and film—in the last five years. She has managed to shift from acting roles into more significant directing roles and into producing. Her first forays into directing came in 2013 and included both an episode of the television series *Southland* (on which she performed as an actor) and the TV movie *Let the Church Say Amen* (BET). She later directed six episodes of *Being Mary Jane*, where she worked with producer Mara Brock Akil (2015); two episodes of *Scandal* and one of *The Catch*, both produced by Shonda Rhimes (2015–16); and one episode of *Insecure*, created by Issa Rae, in 2018. These are only a few of the television episodes that she directed; she also directed for *Greenleaf*, *This Is Us*, and *Pitch*.

While her work prior to the Oscar (for *If Beale Street Could Talk*) was strong, and she worked consistently throughout her career, the Oscar recognition enabled her, like many others, to take advantage of additional opportunities.

In an interview with Sam Sanders from 2019, King relates that the timing of the Oscar—at this pivotal point in her career—enabled her to see that award not as a culmination of her career but as "great currency for the next" (Sanders 2020). And that moment, which came while she was shooting *Watchmen*, did become a "jumping off" point for her and was shortly followed up by her feature-length directorial debut with the critically acclaimed film *One Night in Miami*.

King's career has long been rooted in Black arts and community, and that aesthetic choice came from her grounding in community. She happened to meet Betty Bridges, who had created a community acting school called the Cambridge Academy, and worked there for several years before auditioning for, and being cast in, *227*. The structure of the Cambridge Academy, which was open to all ages, allowed her to work with and observe people with greater experience and to see what it means to work as an actor. While King does not have the extensive stage experience of others I profile here, her early years with Cambridge did include stage acting and in-depth training in acting. As she began her career with Marla Gibbs on the cast of *227*, she grew and developed as an artist. Her immediate influences were some of the most well-known Black directors of the era, including Gerren Keith, Oz Scott, and Whitney LeBlanc, as well as acting luminaries like Beah Richards, Della Reese, and Paul Winfield, in addition to Gibbs, who was her mentor.

Her earliest film work was directed by John Singleton; in fact, she had parts in the trio of Singleton's most famous films of the early 1990s (*Boyz n the Hood*, *Poetic Justice*, and *Higher Learning*). Being cast in *Boyz n the Hood* enabled her to connect with John Singleton (who was on campus at USC the same time she was). In the work on *Poetic Justice*, Singleton invited her to essentially see what went into making a film, which sparked her curiosity and interest in working on both sides of the camera. After doing a lot of film work, she decided to focus more on television. Her motivation was twofold; after playing supporting roles (specifically as the wife of a central character) in *Jerry Maguire*, *Enemy of the State*, and *Ray*, she looked for opportunities to break out of the "wife" character. Television offered her a chance to play different kinds of characters. Her work on *Southland*—in a role that was initially not written for a Black woman— gained critical acclaim, even if it remained under the radar of audiences and Emmy voters.

In 2010, King wrote a piece that was published in *Huffington Post*, calling attention to problems in Emmy nominations and voting. What prompted her to write the essay was years of watching Black actors do excellent work in television that failed to be recognized by the Academy of Television Arts and Sciences. Two very specific things drove her to publish this piece. First was the surprising absence of Alaina Reed Hall from the 2010 Emmy "memoriam"; Hall had acted on *Sesame Street* and on *227*. King initially rationalized Hall's omission from the evening ceremony, thinking that she must have been included on the Daytime, rather than Primetime, show. That changed when she saw a picture of Rutina Wesley, who had attended the awards show, captioned "Regina King enters the 62nd Emmys" (King 2010). Her piece in the *Huffington Post* highlights the dearth of nonwhite actors nominated for Emmys: "there have been only 53 non-white actors nominated for Emmys out of nearly 1,000 possible nominations in the top four acting categories for drama and comedy" (King 2010). From her work in the industry, King recognized both the increase in representation in the late 1980s and 1990s and the decline in Black actors in television programs (and Black-themed programming) in the 2000s.[2]

As her career advanced, she was able to "move with more confidence," and in 2013, she began directing. After consulting with Chris Chulack, who was her director on *Southland*, she applied for, and was accepted into, ABC Studios' directing program. (In part, she chose ABC because of the work that Rhimes was doing on the network.) She shadowed Tom Verica, who was also an actor/director. Her early work included television episodes, movies, and documentary film. Several directing credits later, she was selected to direct *One Night in Miami*. One of the reasons she chose the script was that it was an opportunity for her to be involved in a project that presented "layered Black male characters"; she saw the film as "a love letter about Black men's experience" (Feingold 2020).

Many of King's projects engage themes of race and racial discrimination, crime, and policing; in fact, most of her work since she began work on *American Crime* in 2015 has focused around these themes. In an interview, King said,

> I don't feel like I'm actively looking for these stories, but if the story moves me, and feels like it's rooted in truth, I'm attracted to it. So much of that is part of my experience being Black in America. I can't help but be attracted to it. Five or six things will hit my desk, but that will be the one that my heart says yes.
>
> (Sanders 2020)

In 2019, she signed a multiyear "first look" deal with Netflix through her production company, Royal Ties (Amatulli 2019).

Looking Back and Looking Forward (February 2022)

Since I last wrote about King and Davis, the United States (and the world) have undergone radical transformation. In the summer of 2020, the murders of George Floyd, Breonna Taylor, and Ahmaud Aubrey brought acute attention to the continuing murders of Black people on a large scale. The Black Lives Matter Movement, begun by three Black queer women after the murder of Trayvon Martin in 2012, was reignited, and the summer saw a mass movement with significant protests in cities large and small. That anguish was heightened by the fact that we had entered the COVID-19 pandemic and had spent the spring startled by a highly contagious, novel virus that hospitalized and killed millions worldwide. We were at once awoken to the fragility of our "normal" and were pushed into a new reality. The 2020 presidential election revealed to us how deep-seated white supremacy is in the United States, and we entered 2021 with an attack on US Capitol and the core principles of democracy. We were all, in many ways, shaken to our core.

The pandemic's deep effects have been—as one might expect—more challenging for Black communities. The precarity of Black lives was acutely revealed: blacks were more vulnerable to infection (because they held more "essential" positions, which required direct contact with people), more strongly affected because of health inequities and differential health outcomes, and more vulnerable to lost jobs when businesses closed, to lost living spaces because of income loss, and to lost communities as the virus took lives.

In the midst of this have been cultural shifts that concern the arena of this project, particularly in the televisual world. With movie theatres closed during lockdown, audiences turned to the streaming world in droves as new services—Peacock, CBS/Paramount, Disney+, HBO Max—joined the ranks of Netflix, Hulu, Apple TV+, and Amazon Prime. Isolation accelerated audiences' appetite for streaming services, and those services responded with content. And perhaps the heightened awareness of white supremacy and racism increased audience interest and support of Black-themed programming. Audiences watched the Shondaland production *Bridgerton* in part because of her casting of Black characters in Regency England, particularly Queen Charlotte;[3] it became Netflix's fifth-highest viewed program (as of January 2021). The question remains whether *Bridgerton*'s popularity was indicative of a turn in audience interest: Did it signal that audiences were seeking more diversity in their viewing, and is narrowcasting declining? And yet, in spite of its huge popularity, *Bridgerton* failed to gain even a single Golden Globe nomination in 2021, as did *Insecure* and Michaela Cole's *I May Destroy You*, both critical successes and popular with audiences (Romero 2021).

As we look to the future, we see some emerging creators from the next generation; some of them have already begun to shift and shape the industry in interesting ways. We will focus here on two, Janelle Monáe and Marsai Martin, but they are not alone in bringing new Black stories to audiences.

Janelle Monáe: Multidisciplinary Artist

Janelle Monáe is important in the next generation of creators; she is, in many ways, a younger version of others who moved from a career in music to one in the televisual and film arts (Ethel Waters and Queen Latifah, specifically). Monáe's early years featured work in the Coterie Theater's Young Playwrights' Round Table, and she studied for a time at the American Musical and Dramatic Academy (AMDA). She emerged in the early 2000s as an enigmatic artist whose presentation—whether as her android alter ego Cindi Mayweather or dressed in androgynous black and white—challenged racialized gender norms and was significantly different from the other Black women recording artists of the time period. She created her own record label and studio, Wondaland, which has become a kind of refuge as well as a studio for new and emerging artists (Wortham 2018). She began acting; she was drawn to the script for *Moonlight* and followed up that performance with a role in *Hidden Figures*.

Monáe is not afraid to embrace politics through her art. In her early work, this came through (although somewhat veiled) her alter ego; now, she is much more open about her political commitments. Of course, her music is one way this happens. Her 2017 album *Dirty Computer* embraces women's sexuality and desire (including same-gender desire) and Black political action, concluding with a future vision of the United States that is truly inclusive. This is her first album where she does not "hide" behind Mayweather. As *New York Times* cultural critic Jenna Wortham says, "Mayweather was a proxy for all the things about Monáe that made others uncomfortable, like her androgyny, her opaque sexual identity, her gender fluidity—her defiance of easy categorization" (Wortham 2018). In 2015 she released a single, "Hell You Talmbout," which is a musical tribute to Black people murdered by police. In 2021, she revised this project with the African American Policy Forum by focusing on Black women, with a call-and-response "say her name" after each woman's name is called; bringing in additional artists, scholars, and activists; and adding new names.

Monáe has owned her own record label since 2015, and prior to establishing Wondaland, she worked with Sean Combs's Bad Boy label—so she understands the value of controlling the production of one's art. In 2018, she founded the organization Fem the Future, a collaboration with Belvedere vodka to connect Black women creators with each other and to create programs for girls through after-school and summer camp opportunities in music and arts. Its first project, "A Beautiful Future," featured three Black women directors and shorts that are posted on YouTube. While many projects were scaled back or put on hold during the height of the COVID-19 pandemic, Fem the Future plans to continue its projects, especially those focused on young creators, in the coming year.

She Got Next: Marsai Martin

Finally, I turn to the young creator Marsai Martin. At age seventeen, Martin has been an actor for much of her life, having emerged on Kenya Barris's *black-ish* in 2014. While viewers watched her grow up (and develop as an actor) on the sitcom, Martin has not been content to be "just" a child actor. At age ten, she pitched a movie idea that became the film *Little*, which also starred Martin and Issa Rae and is Martin's first producing credit. She established a production company, Genius Productions, which signed a deal with Universal in 2019. She is currently executive producer on two new series, *Free to Fall* (postproduction) and *Saturdays* (filming).

Martin has been mentored by Kenya Barris, the creator and executive producer of *black-ish*; it was to Barris that Martin first pitched her idea for *Little*, and he helped her develop the pitch. She is also strongly supported by her parents, who are the president and vice president of Genius Productions. *Saturdays* will be broadcast by Disney and "tells the story of a girl who is battling sickle cell disease all while pursuing her passion for roller skating" (Boateng 2021). The production company is focused on creating film and television programming that features the variety of Black girlhood. Martin is also committed to developing programming that highlights Black communities and cultures positively; she has said that "I don't like to do Black trauma" (Carter 2021).

Martin was nominated for multiple awards for *Little*, including the NAACP Image Award for Outstanding Supporting Actress in a Motion Picture and

Outstanding Breakthrough Performance in a Motion Picture. She has also been nominated for SAG awards for her work on *black-ish*. Clearly, Martin is poised to continue to make a significant contribution in Hollywood, engaging with other Black creators to produce projects that shift both representation and the people who develop those representations.

Conclusion

We can look at these twenty-first-century developments in both network television and cable as the culmination of decades of work by Blacks in the film and television industry to make significant progress in advancing more complex, interesting, and realistic portraits of Black life in the United States. Today, the combination of streaming and pay television services, as well as cable channels offering original series, provides the bulk of the programming that portrays the diversity of Black life. While network television works to show us an integrated, sometimes assimilationist world (the happy, multicultural world where race doesn't matter all that much now, even if it used to historically), streaming services like Netflix, Hulu, and Amazon need worry less about advertising revenue and programs in the top of the ratings. Between streaming services, where many people binge the content of a season in a few days, and the ubiquity of DVR recording, which means many people do not watch programs when they air, the old models of television are beginning to break down. They haven't gone away, at least not yet; but Oprah is less reliant on broad appeal to large audiences to gather support for *Queen Sugar*, and we have begun to see the results of Shonda Rhimes's move to Netflix, where any and all new content she develops will be broadcast (Koblin 2017).

It is also clear that some of the best work on television is not being broadcast on the Big Four networks.[4] Of the programs nominated for Emmy awards for Outstanding Comedy Series in 2021, only one of the eight was broadcast on a major network (*black-ish*, on ABC); of the eight Outstanding Drama Series nominations, only one was for a program broadcast on a major network, while two were Netflix original series, and one each were on HBO, FX, Amazon Prime, and Disney+. Winners in both categories were from streaming (Apple TV+ and Netflix). This continues a trend that began in 2014, when original programming from Netflix was first nominated for Emmy awards (Academy 2018).

This convergence of technological advances and decades of Black women showrunners mentoring younger Black women artists has finally accomplished what Hattie McDaniel thought she would be able to do when she signed on for the radio version of *The Beulah Show*. We have moved from the incremental steps that typified the earlier decades of television, when access to production, direction, and writing roles was extremely limited for Black artists. For all of their various accolades, the talented Black women actors who strove to broaden the representations of Black women on television made very little progress until they were able to gain experience in directing, writing, and producing television. It has taken all of this, and the intersectional feminist perspectives advocated by many of the women who have emerged in the post-*Different World* era, to have finally succeeded in presenting Black verisimilitude.

Developments in the first two decades of the twenty-first century have allowed for programming aimed at Black audiences—sometimes specifically Black women—to emerge and be sustained, even if in a somewhat limited fashion. The examples here also demonstrate that it is not enough to be "good." Television still regards Black-themed work as "risky," and while some networks are open to putting money into new or continuing shows that take Black lives and Black experiences seriously, these opportunities are still relatively few, and networks are much more willing to take a chance on work that speaks to a "larger" (white) audience. Networks, whether broadcast, cable, or subscription, still operate from a position in which whiteness is normalized and rendered unmarked in various representations. Their understanding of "diversity" is often only skin deep, of which the experiences of Issa Rae and her venture with ABC are but one example.

Networks are also reluctant to take risks on "unknowns"—or at least, unknown to them. Black women writers, directors, and producers who have a "track record," who are known to network decision-makers, are more likely to be successful at pitching an idea. It is also true that in spite of their experience, successfully creating content for the televisual world can still be a challenge, especially financially. If not for Kelsey Grammer's being sold on *Girlfriends*, that show might not have been made—and Mara Brock Akil's career, and the television landscape, might have looked very different. Even when all of the pieces are in place, getting a series picked up and broadcast is still a *negotiation*.

For the most part, though, the inclusion of Black women among the ranks of writers, directors, producers, and executive producers has broadened the kinds of representations of Blackness that Black audiences in particular have long desired. While there are still simple, two-dimensional Black characters within the television landscape, there is also now a significant number of *other* representations, ones that show a diversity and complexity of Black life in the United States. While negotiating respectability politics and the stark whiteness of the industry, Black women are making some headway in shifting representations. The success of Quinta Brunson's *Abbott Elementary* (ABC) is a bright spot in network TV in 2022.

Mentorship remains vital to increasing the numbers of Black women in television production. It is the case in several of the examples here that a foot in the door for one person led to an open door for the next generation. Brock Akil, who was mentored like other Black women showrunners during the 1990s, has continued to be productive in television. Debbie Allen's move from *Fame* to *A Different World*, facilitated by her skill and reputation in theatre and film as well as television, made space and opened a door for Yvette Lee Bowser, who went from working on *A Different World* to producing *Living Single*. These two programs were influential beyond their popularity at the time; Issa Rae recalls watching both shows when she was young as inspiration for her own work (Villareal 2015).

The growth in outlets—particularly streaming services—has increased opportunities for Black women creators to have their work produced and broadcast/streamed. These expansions in opportunities also translate into expansions in the types of Blackness represented in the televisual. And while multiracial ensemble programming continues, particularly in primetime on network television, it is vitally important that television moves away from the "controlling images" that have been present throughout much of the history of the medium. That it takes Oprah Winfrey's media ownership to afford the opportunity for a *Queen Sugar* demonstrates that television shows that reflect the multiplicity of Blackness still require investment from those who understand that multiplicity and the importance of seeing those varied images on the small screen. When viewers can see Black stories as universal even while being particular, we are able to tap into the potentially transformative power of television.

Notes

Introduction

1   The term "respectability politics" emerged from the work of Evelyn Brooks Higginbotham, through her 1993 book on Black church women in the late nineteenth and early twentieth century (*Righteous Discontent: The Women's Movement in the Black Baptist Church, 1880–1920*). While the phrase Higginbotham used was "the politics of respectability," this concept has carried through in Black feminist scholarship since the mid-1990s, and become a significant heuristic particularly since the advent of Black Lives Matter. In part, academics and activists have taken up this context because of the failure of the politics of respectability, which promised access to the privileges of full citizenship if Black people were "respectable," mimicking hegemonic middle-class ideas of family and propriety.

2   In this, I am deriving my own Black feminist perspective in part from Alice Walker's definition of *womanism*, but also considering the long history of Black women writers, thinkers, and activists who recognize that Black *feminist* concerns are concerns of a whole people.

Chapter 1

1   The cakewalk was a performance tradition that began during slavery. It was designed as an opportunity for slaves to perform for white audiences, and the "prize" was a cake. It mimicked nineteenth-century ballroom dances, particularly promenade or line-type dances. Cakewalk persisted as an element of the nineteenth-century minstrel show and into the twentieth century through both Black musical (such as Will Marion Cook's *Clorindy, or the Origin of the Cakewalk*, 1898) and vaudeville.

2   While *Beulah* never made it into the Nielsen top-thirty, Brooks and Marsh state that "*Beulah* was still receiving high ratings in September 1953 when it went off the air because Miss Beavers decided to leave the role" (Brooks and Marsh 2007, 129).

3   "Signifyin'" refers to an African American discursive practice that plays with meanings. Theorized through the figure of the Signifying Monkey by Henry Louis Gates, I use the term here to refer to the dissembling quality of performance practices that disguise their intent.

4   I am including here only the years that featured Black women playing Beulah; the original program, with its white actors, began in 1945.

5   Particularly here, the NAACP, and its chairman at the time, Walter White. White and McDaniel had a long-running conflict over Hollywood representations and the actors who played these roles (Watts 2005).

6   Sam McDaniel's marginalia in the scripts only notes that sections were cut; whether these cuts came from the writers/directors/producers or from Hattie McDaniel remains unknown.

7   The "dozens" is an African American custom, usually engaged in by men, of insults and trash talk. This verbal sparring continues until one competitor does not have a better comeback.

8   Schwartz developed *Gilligan's Island* and *The Brady Bunch,* among other programs.

9   The transition between McDaniel and Beavers is a little complicated. McDaniel filmed six episodes in 1951 but suffered a stroke on top of her diabetes and advanced heart disease. ABC shelved the six episodes with the expectation that McDaniel's health would improve and hired Beavers to take over. They broadcast McDaniel's episodes at the end of the second season, with hopes that she would return for the third season, but before she could return, McDaniel was diagnosed with advanced breast cancer (Watts 2005). When McDaniel did not return, Beavers continued in the role.

10   One of the critiques to which McDaniel was responding in her letter was an accusation of her as an "Uncle Tom."

Chapter 2

1   There are generally two models of how actors take up characters. In one, which comes from the Stanislavsky acting technique, actors work to "become" the character, so that the actor's self disappears and we only see the playwright's character on the stage. The other technique is one in which the actor "shows" the character. It is this type of performance that I think typified the Black-in-Blackface

minstrelsy, the "signifyn'" of the cakewalk, and the performance of actors like Anderson while performing these kinds of roles.

2   The year 1968 top-ten shows were: *Rowan & Martin's Laugh-in*; *Gomer Pyle, USMC*; *Bonanza*; *Mayberry RFD*; *Family Affair*; *Gunsmoke*; *Julia*; *Dean Martin Show*; *Here's Lucy*; *Beverly Hillbillies*.

3   The "sapphire" character—so named for the *Amos 'N' Andy* character—is sometimes thought of as a variation of the jezebel character, but sapphire is less sexualized (jezebel is specifically sexualized). What typifies the sapphire character is more domineering, critical, emasculating, and she can also be the "Angry Black Woman" stereotype as well.

4   In 1950, Juanita Hall won the Tony for Best Performance by a Featured Actress in a Musical, making her the first Black Tony winner and first Black woman Tony winner.

5   Redlining was the process of institutions delineating areas in which they would not invest. Most importantly here, this was a common practice among banks, who would refuse to lend to Black prospective homeowners who lived in Black neighborhoods. In addition to these practices, the practice of using real estate covenants to prevent the sale of homes to minority buyers, and the refusal of apartment managers to rent to Blacks, were common institutional barriers to Black homeownership and neighborhood integration. See, for example, Bill Dedman (May 1, 1988), "The Color of Money" (*The Atlanta Journal-Constitution*); Angela Hanks, Danyelle Solomon, and Christian E. Weller, "Systematic Inequality," Center for American Progress (https://www.americanprogress.org/issues/race/reports/2018/02/21/447051/systematic-inequality/).

6   I say this as someone who as a young child of about Corey's age lived in an integrated community. In retrospect, perhaps, I can recount several incidences from my childhood that were examples of racism that my parents explained to me as such. Others who also were children during this time could reference similar incidents.

7   This is likely a reference to Edward Brooke, who was a Black man elected to the senate from Massachusetts in 1966 and took office in 1967. He would be the third Black senator in the US Senate, technically, but the first one since Reconstruction.

8   During this period, Julia is not the only single parent on television; notably, *Family Affair*, which ran from 1966 to 1971, features a man who takes in his orphaned nieces and nephew and essentially functions as a kind of single parent (Brooks and Marsh 2007, 449).

Chapter 3

1 *Get Christie Love* was a short-lived (one season) police procedural starring Teresa Graves as a Black policewoman; Clifton Davis's *That's My Mama* ran for two seasons. These programs, along with *The Richard Pryor Show* and *Benson*, would constitute the Black-themed programming during the time that *Good Times* was on the air, and up to 1980.

2 Melvin Van Peebles is probably most famous for his classic film that kicked off the blaxploitation era, *Sweet Sweetback's Baadasssss Song*.

3 My interest in representations of Black families, and of Black peoples as a whole, emerges from Alice Walker's definition of *womanist* (Walker 1983).

4 The "coon" character, which originated in Blackface minstrelsy with the character of "old zip coon." In general, a "coon" refers to a character "presenting the Negro as amusement object and black buffoon. […] the pure coons emerged as … unreliable, crazy, lazy, subhuman creatures good for nothing more than eating watermelons, stealing chickens, shooting craps, or butchering the English language" (Bogle 1996, 7–8).

5 Curiously, this will be the episode discussed at the end of this chapter that was chosen as the episode to reprise in 2019 with "Live in front of a Studio Audience," a program reprising several Norman Lear comedies.

Chapter 4

1 For example, Zook sees *Cosby* as having a "message of a color-blind society" (31); Donald Bogle relates that the show "had its critics, who complained that the series was too soft and safe" (2001, 294–5); these included reviewers from *the Village Voice, New York Magazine*, and a study by scholars at the University of Massachusetts.

2 The term "postnetwork" was coined by Amanda Lotz in her 2007 book, *The Television Will Be Revolutionized* (New York, NY: New York University Press, 2007).

3 The Links, Inc. is a professional Black women's organization that was founded in Philadelphia in 1946. "It is one of the nation's oldest and largest volunteer service organizations of extraordinary women who are committed to enriching, sustaining, and ensuring the culture and economic survival of African Americans and other persons of African ancestry." www.linksinc.org

4 A "talent holding deal" is a contract between a studio and an actor while the studio is looking to develop a program or film. As a studio, Warner was interested in working with both Latifah and Fields on developing a new

program. While the studio was producing the program, the program was being produced for the Fox network.

5   Among the Black-themed shows on the Big Three in the early 2000s were the short-lived *Whoopi* and *My Wife and Kids*.

Chapter 5

1   The work requirement meant that welfare recipients were required to work for their welfare check. They were not paid an actual salary, nor were they given benefits.

2   Rhimes's work, and both shows, are mentioned in Janelle Monáe's song "Django Jane" on her *Dirty Computer* album, pointing to the popularity of both *Scandal* and *How to Get Away with Murder* among younger Black audiences. For a critique of the "flatness" of the character Olivia Pope, as well as the political implications, see Brandon Maxwell's blog post for *The Feminist Wire* (Maxwell 2013); see also Tanisha Ford's essay in *The Atlantic* (Ford 2018).

3   Kenya Barris's *black-ish* will hit the eight-season mark with its 2021–2 season.

4   Franchesca Ramsey has also successfully moved from the world of social media to television, as a contributing writer to Larry Wilmore's Comedy Central show and appearances on MTV.

Conclusion

1   Fans started a "Walk like Annalise Keating" Tiktok challenge in Fall of 2021. See, for example, George, Rachel, *Atlanta Black Star* https://atlantablackstar.com/2021/10/29/thats-a-little-f-d-up-of-yall-viola-davis-reacts-to-viral-walking-like-annalise-challenge-on-tiktok/

2   The 2021 Emmys saw lots of Black actors nominated—but no winners, at least in the acting category.

3   There was some chatter about whether or not Queen Charlotte had African ancestry, based on reports about her at the time. Romano, Aja, Vox.com https://www.vox.com/22215076/bridgerton-race-racism-historical-accuracy-alternate-history; Borwn, DeNeen L. *The Washington Post* https://www.washingtonpost.com/news/retropolis/wp/2018/05/15/meghan-markle-queen-charlotte-and-the-wedding-of-britains-first-mixed-race-royal/

4   ABC continues to engage Black audiences; winter 2022 has brought three Black-themed programs to audiences (*Queens, Abbott Elementary,* and a Black-cast reboot of *The Wonder Years*). *Abbott Elementary* was created by Quinta Brunson,

who is also an executive producer and writer and plays the main character. Tim Story, best known for the *Barbershop* films, is an executive producer of *Queens*, while Lee Daniels is an executive producer of *The Wonder Years*. *Abbott Elementary* has met critical acclaim and an enthusiastic audience, with the second episode marking "ABC's strongest comedy telecast of new or returning series in nearly two years, since the April 8, 2020, series finale of *Modern Family*" (Andreeva 2022). ABC's commitment to bringing Black-themed programming to audiences marks it as somewhat unusual among the major networks; their gauge of what today's audiences want seems to be paying off for them. It may be an indicator that audiences are indeed interested in Black-themed programming, especially for strong comedies in these stressful contemporary times.

Reference List

Academy, The Motion Picture. 2018. "The Emmys." Retrieved from http://www.emmys.com/awards.

Acham, Christine. 2004. *Revolution Televised: Prime Time and the Struggle for Black Power*. Minneapolis: University of Minnesota Press.

Allen, Debbie. 2011. *Debbie Allen/Interviewer: S.J. Abramson*. Archive of American Television, Emmys.com.

Amatulli, Jenna. 2019. "Regina King Inks First-Look, Multi-year Deal with Netflix and Fans Love It." *Huffington Post*, May 5. Retrieved from https://www.huffpost.com/entry/regina-king-netflix-first-look_n_5ccb035be4b0d123954fc15b.

Amos, John. 2014. *Archive of American Television/Interviewer: N. Harrington*.

Anderson, Lisa M. 1995. "From Blackface to 'Genuine Negroes': Nineteenth Century Minstrelsy and the Icon of the 'Negro.'" *Theatre Research International*, 21 (1), 17–23.

Anderson, Lisa M. 1997. *Mammies No More: The Changing Image of Black Women on Stage and Screen*. Lanham, MD: Rowman and Littlefield Publishers.

Andreeva, Nellie. 2020. "Mara Brock Akil Inks Overall Deal with Netflix as Steamer Sets Premier Date for Her Series 'Girlfriends.'" *Deadline*. Retrieved from https://deadline.com/2020/09/mara-brock-akil-inks-overall-deal-netflix-girlfriends-premiere-date-1234573545/.

Andreeva, Nellie. 2022. "'Abbott Elementary' Episode 2 Nabs ABC's Strongest Comedy Ratings Since 'Modern Family' Finale in MP35." *Deadline*, February 23. Retrieved from https://deadline.com/2022/02/abbott-elementary-episode-2-best-ratings-modern-family-finale-mp35-1234958745/.

Ausiello, Michael. 2019. "*Grey's Anatomy* Renewed for *Two* More Seasons at ABC as Ellen Pompeo Extends Contract Until 2021." *TV Line*.

Bean, Annamarie. 2001. "Black Minstrelsy and Double Inversion, circa 1890." In *African American Performance and Theater History: A Critical Reader*. Edited by Harry J. Elam, Jr. and David Krasner. New York: Oxford University Press.

Bean, Annamarie, James V. Hatch, and Brooks McNamara (Eds). 1996. *Inside the Minstrel Mask: Readings in Nineteenth-Century Blackface Minstrelsy*. Hanover, NH: Wesleyan University Press.

Boateng, Grace. 2021. "Marsai Martin: How the Actress and Producer Is Moving the Culture Forward." *Forward Times*, March 24. Retrieved from https://forwardtimes.com/marsai-martin-how-the-actress-and-producer-is-pushing-the-culture-forward/.

Bobo, Jacqueline. 1995. *Black Women as Cultural Readers*. New York: Columbia University Press.

Bogle, Donald. 1996. *Toms, Coons, Mulattoes, Mammies and Bucks: An Interpretive History of Blacks in American Films*. 3rd ed. New York: Continuum.

Bogle, Donald. 2001. *Primetime Blues: African Americans on Network Television*. New York: Farrar, Straus and Giroux.

Bogle, Donald. 2011. *Heat Wave: The Life and Career of Ethel Waters*. New York: Harper.

Borwn, DeNeen L. 2018. "Meghan Markle, Queen Charlotte, and the Wedding of Britain's First Mixed-Race Royal." *The Washington Post*, May 19. Retrieved from https://www.washingtonpost.com/news/retropolis/wp/2018/05/15/meghan-markle-queen-charlotte-and-the-wedding-of-britains-first-mixed-race-royal/.

Brooks, Tim, and Earle Marsh. 2007. *The Complete Directory to Prime Time Network TV Shows*. 9th ed. New York: Ballantine.

Bultema, James A. 2013. *Guardians of Angels: A History of the Los Angeles Police Department*. Los Angeles, CA: Infinity Publishing.

Byrd, Ayana, and Lori Tharps. 2014. *Hair Story: Untangling the Roots of Black Hair in America*. Revised ed. New York: St. Martin's Griffin.

Carroll, Diahann, and Ross Firestone. 1986. *Diahann: An Autobiography*. Boston: Little, Brown.

Carter, Terry Jr. 2021. "Marsai Martin Revealed What It's Really Like Working on 'Black-ish' with Tracee Ellis Ross and Anthony Anderson." *Buzzfeed*, June 3. Retrieved from https://www.buzzfeed.com/terrycarter/marsai-martin-blackish-spirit-untamed-interview.

Chism, Monique M. 2005. "Rolle, Esther." In *Black Women in America*. 2nd ed. Edited by D.C. Hine. New York: Oxford University Press (online version).

Coleman, Robin R. Means. 2000. *African American Viewers and the Black Situation Comedy: Situating Racial Humor*. New York: Routledge.

Coleman, Robin R. Means, and Alvin M. Cavalcante. 2013. "Two Different Worlds: Television as a Producer's Medium." In *Watching While Black: Centering the Television of Black Audiences*. Edited by E. Pierson and R.M. Coleman. New Brunswick, NJ: Rutgers University Press.

Collins, Patricia Hill. 1990. *Black Feminist Thought: Knowledge, Consciousness, and the Politics of Empowerment*. Boston: Unwin Hyman.

Collins, Patricia Hill. 2005. *Black Sexual Politics: African Americans, Gender, and the New Racism*. New York: Routledge.

Davis, Viola. 2016. *Delivering Democracy Lecture/Interviewer: K. Covington*. Phoenix, AZ: Arizona State University/Pilgrim Rest Baptist Church.

Dill, Bonnie Thornton. 1994. *Across the Boundaries of Race and Class: An Exploration of Work and Family among Black Female Domestic Servants*. New York: Garland.

Elam, Harry J. and David Krasner (Eds). 2001. *African American Performance and Theatre History: A Critical Reader*. Cary, NC: Oxford University Press.

Ely, Melvin Patrick. 1991. *The Adventures of Amos 'N' Andy: A Social History of an American Phenomenon*. New York: The Free Press.

Entman, Robert M., and Andrew Rojecki. 2000. *The Black Image in the White Mind: Media and Race in America*. Chicago: University of Chicago Press.

Erigha, Maryann. 2019. *The Hollywood Jim Crow: The Racial Politics of the Movie Industry*. New York: New York University Press.

Feingold, Scott. 2020. "Regina King—'One Night in Miami.'" *Awards Chatter* [podcast]. awardschatter.simplecast.com. November 20.

Fellner, Jamie. 2000. *Punishment and Prejudice: Racial Disparities in the War on Drugs*. Retrieved from https://www.hrw.org/legacy/reports/2000/usa/index.htm#TopOfPage.

Ford, Tanisha C. 2018. "The Episode That Captured the Best and Worst of *Scandal*." *The Atlantic*, April 19. Retrieved from https://www.theatlantic.com/entertainment/archive/2018/04/scandal-series-finale-price-of-free-and-fair-elections/558299/.

Foreman, Ellen. 1980. "The Negro Ensemble Company: A Transcendent Vision." In *The Theatre of Black Americans: A Collection of Critical Essays*. Edited by E. Hill. New York: Applause Books.

Gray, Herman. 2004. *Watching Race: Television and the Struggle for Blackness*. 2nd ed. Minneapolis: University of Minnesota Press.

Gray, Herman. 2005. "The Politics of Representation in Network Television." In *Channeling Blackness: Studies on Television and Race in Media*. Edited by D.M. Hunt. New York: Oxford University Press.

Haggins, Bambi. 2007. *Laughing Mad: The Black Comic Persona in Post-Soul America*. New Brunswick, NJ: Rutgers University Press.

Hall, Carla. 1993. "Back from a Different World: Director Debbie Allen, Making Each Step Count." *The Washington Post*, May 8, B1.

Hall, Stuart. 1993. "Encoding, Decoding." In *The Cultural Studies Reader*. 2nd ed. Edited by Simon During, 508–17. London: Routledge.

Harrison, Paul Carter. 1972. *The Drama of Nommo: Black Theatre in the African Continuum*. New York: Grove Press.

Hay, Samuel. 1994. *African American Theatre: An Historical and Critical analysis*. Cary, NC: Oxford University Press.

Hill, Errol. 1987. *The Theatre of Black Americans: A Collection of Critical Essays*. New York: Applause.

Hinton, David (Director). 1988. *The Making of a Legend: Gone with the Wind* [Film]. Warner Brothers.

hooks, bell. 1992. *Black Looks: Race and Representation*. Boston: South End Press.

Hunt, Darnell M. 2005. "Black Content, White Control." In *Channeling Blackness: Studies on Race and Television in America*. Edited by Darnell M. Hunt. New York: Oxford University Press.

Hunt, Stacey Wilson. 2011. "Grey's Anatomy's Shonda Rhimes Turns Up the Heat in a New Series 'Scandal.'" *Hollywood Reporter*. Retrieved from https://www.hollywoodreporter.com/news/greys-anatomys-shonda-rhimes-turns-205721.

Jewell, K. Sue. 1993. *From Mammy to Miss America and Beyond: Cultural Images and the Shaping of US Social Policy*. New York: Routledge.

Kameir, Rawiya. 2016. "How Mara Brock Akil Plans to Save TV." *The Fader*, April 22. Retrieved from http://www.thefader.com/2016/04/22/mara-brock-akil-interview-warner-bros.

Kanter, Hal, Howard Leeds, and Arthur Julian. 1948. *The Beulah Show, ep. 78*. [script for radio show]. Hattie and Sam McDaniel Papers, (F. 8). Margaret Herrick Library, Special Collections.

King, Regina. 2010. "The Emmys: As White as Ever." *Huffington Post*. September 3.

Koblin, John. 2017. "Netflix Signs Shonda Rhimes in Counterpunch to ABC and Disney." *The New York Times*, August 14. Retrieved from https://www.nytimes.com/2017/08/14/business/media/shonda-rhimes-netflix-deal.html.

Lorde, Audre. 1983. *Sister/Outsider: Essays and Speeches*. Trumansburg, NY: Crossing Press.

Lorde, Audre. 2009. *I Am Your Sister: Colleged and Unpublished Writings of Audre Lorde*. Edited by Rudolph P. Byrd, Johnetta Betsch Cole, and Beverly Guy Sheftall. New York: Oxford University Press.

Margulies, Lee. 1977. "Why Florida Left: The Bad Times at Good Times." *Los Angeles Times*.

Margulies, Lee. 1978. "Back to 'Good Times': Esther Rolle: Coming Home." *Los Angeles Times*, May 19.

Maxwell, Brandon. 2013. "Olivia Pope and the Scandal of Representation." Retrieved from https://thefeministwire.com/2013/02/olivia-pope-and-the-scandal-of-representation/.

McDaniel, Hattue. 1947. *Letter to Hedda Hopper*, March 29. Hattie and Sam McDaniel Papers (f.2296 Letters). Margaret Herrick Library, Special Collection.

Means Coleman, Robin. 1998. *African American Viewers and the Black Situation Comedy: Situating Racial Humor*. New York and London: Garland Publishing.

Mitchell, Elvis. 1988. "Television: A for Effort." *Rolling Stone* 524 (April 21, 1988), 32–33.

Mitchell, Loften. 1967. *Black Drama: The Story of the American Negro in the Theatre*. New York: Hawthorne Books.

Mock, Brentin. "The Gentrification of City-Based Sitcoms." *Citylab.com*. Retrieved from https://www.citylab.com/life/2017/01/the-gentrification-of-city-based-sitcoms/513302/.

Morrison, Toni. 1992. *Playing in the Dark: Whiteness and the Literary Imagination*. Cambridge, MA: Harvard University Press.

Nama, Adilifu. 2008. *Black Space: Imagining Race in Science Fiction Film*. Austin, TX: University of Texas Press.

Newman, Katherine S. 2000. *No Shame in My Game: The Working Poor in the Inner City*. New York: Vintage.

Obie, Brooke. 2019. "Erika Alexander Explains 'Friends' Success vs. 'Living Single': "They Have the Complexion for the Protection." *Shadow and Act*, March 8. Retrieved from https://www.shadowandact.com/erika-alexander-explains-friends-success-vs-living-single-they-have-the-complexion-for-the-protection.

Patton, Tracy Owens. 2006. "Hey Girl, Am I More than My Hair?: African American Women and Their Strubbles with Beauty, Body Image, and Hair." *NWSA Journal*, 18 (2), 24–51.

PBS, M. (Producer). 2013. "Diahann Carroll."

Petty, Miriam J. 2016. *Stealing the Show: African American Performers and Audiences in 1930s Hollywood*. Oakland, CA: University of California Press.

Press, Associated. 2019. "Viola Davis Determined to Go above and beyond on Diversity." *The New York Times*, June 24. Retrieved from https://www.nytimes.com/aponline/2019/06/24/arts/ap-us-film-viola-davis.html?searchResultPositi on=14.

Rae, Issa. 2016. @IssaRae Presents. Retrieved from www.issarae.com.

Regester, Charlene B. 2010. *African American Actresses: The Struggle for Visibility, 1900–1960*. Bloomington: Indiana University Press.

Richards, David. 1986. "The Latest Stage of Esther Rolle: 'Good Times' and Bad: And Now, 'Raisin' & the Hope of Rediscovery." *The Washington Post*, November 11.

Riggs, Marlon (Writer). 1992. *Color Adjustment*. In: California Newsreel.

Romano, Aja. 2021. "The Debate over Bridgerton and Race." *Vox.com*. Retrieved from Vox.com https://www.vox.com/22215076/bridgerton-race-racism-historical-accuracy-alternate-history.

Romero, Ariana. 2021. "*Bridgerton* Was Shut out of the Golden Globes. It's Much Worse Than a Simple Snub." *Refinery29*, February 23. Retrieved from https://www.refinery29.com/en-us/2021/02/10291823/bridgerton-golden-globes-nomination-snub-racist.

Ruskin, Coby (Writer). 1968. Paint Your Waggedorn [Television]. In *Julia*: 20th Century Fox.

Sanders, Sam. 2020. *It's Been a Minute*, interview with Regina King [podcast], August 7. NPR.

Simpson, Kelly. 2012. "A Southern Califorina Dream Deferred: Racial Covenants in Los Angeles." Retrieved from https://www.kcet.org/history-society/a-southern-california-dream-deferred-racial-covenants-in-los-angeles.

Smith-Shomade, Beretta E. 2002. *Shaded Lives: African American Women and Television*. New Brunswick, NH: Rutgers University Press.

Smye, Rachel. 2015. "Viola Davis, on Finding Creative Space in TV with No Limitations." *The New York Times*, August 25.

Stanley, Alessandra. 2014. "Wrought in Rhimes's Image." *The New York Times*, September 18.

Steiner, Tobias. 2015. "Under the Macroscope: Convergence in the US Television Market between 2000 and 2014." *Image*, 22.

Taylor, April. 2014. "The Creator of 'Good Times' Is Back with a Vengeance after Being Blackballed by Hollywood." Retrieved from http://financialjuneteenth.com/the-creator-of-good-times-is-back-with-a-vengeance-after-being-blackballed-by-hollywood/.

Taylor, Yuval, and Jake Austen. 2012. *Darkest America: Black Minstrelsy from Slavery to Hip-Hop*. New York: W. W. Norton.

Thompson, Lisa B. 2009. *Beyond the Black Lady: Sexuality and the New African American Middle Class*. Urbana and Chicago: University of Illinois Press.

Toll, Robert. 1974. *Blacking Up: The Minstrel Show in Nineteenth Century America*. New York: Oxford University Press.

Ugwu, Reggie. 2018. "Steve McQueen and Viola Davis on Hollywood, Race and Power." *The New York Times*, November 15.

Unknown (Writer). 2018. "Queen Sugar Season Finale Special." In: Warner Bros. Entertainment.

Viera, Bene. 2013. "Why Living Single Is the Blueprint." *Vibe.com*. Retrieved from https://www.vibe.com/2013/09/why-living-single-is-the-blueprint.

Villareal, Yvonne. 2015. "'Misadventures of Awkward Black Girl' Puts Issa Rae in a Cool Position." *Los Angeles Times*. Retrieved from http://www.latimes.com/books/jacketcopy/la-ca-jc-issa-rae-20150208-story.html.

Walker, Alice. 1983. *In Search of Our Mother's Gardens*. San Diego: Harcourt Brace Jovanovich.

Wallace, Michelle. 1990. "Variations on Negation and the Heresy of Black Feminist Creativity." In *Reading Black, Reading Feminist: A Critical Anthology*. Edited by H.L. Gates. New York: Meridian.

Wallace, Michelle. 1995. *Black Popular Culture*. Edited by Gina Dent. Seattle: Bay Press.

Wallace, Michelle. 2004. *Dark Designs and Visual Culture*. Durham: Duke University Press.

Warner, Kristen J. 2015. *The Cultural Politics of Colorblind TV Casting*. New York: Routledge.

Warner, Kristen J. 2017. "In the Time of Plastic Representation." *Film Quarterly*, 71 (2), 32–7. Retrieved from https://www.jstor.org/stable/26413860.

Watts, Jill. 2005. *Hattie McDaniel: Black Ambition, White Hollywood*. New York: Amistad Books.

Weitz, Rose. 2001. "Women and Their Hair: Seeking Power through Resistance and Accommodation." *Gender and Society*, 15 (5), 667–86.

Wilkerson, Isabel. 2010. *The Warmth of Other Suns: The Epic Story of America's Great Migration*. New York: Vintage.

Wortham, Jenna. 2015. "The Misadventures of Issa Rae." *The New York Times Magazine*, August 4. Retrieved from https://www.nytimes.com/2015/08/09/magazine/the-misadventures-of-issa-rae.html.

Wortham, Jenna. 2018. "How Janelle Monáe Found Her Voice." *The New York Times Magazine*, April 19. Retrieved from https://www.nytimes.com/2018/04/19/magazine/how-janelle-monae-found-her-voice.html

Zook, Krystal Brent. 1999. *Color by Fox: The Fox Network and the Revolution in Black Television*. New York: Oxford University Press.

Index